Cornelius Ryan: D-Day War Reporter

The writer behind *The Longest Day*

& *A Bridge Too Far*

Dominic Phelan

Copyright © Dominic Phelan 2014
(Revised edition 2015)
All rights reserved

CONTENTS

	Prologue	i
1	Dublin 1920	7
2	London 1941	15
3	D-Day 1944	18
4	France 1944	22
5	Germany 1945	28
6	Japan 1945-46	31
7	USA 1947-49	36
8	New Frontiers – 1950s	39
9	The Longest Day 1959	48
10	Cold War 1960-69	56
11	Battling Cancer 1970-74	68
12	Reporter or Historian?	76

Prologue
6th June 1944

As his B-26 bomber turned towards home, 24-year-old war correspondent Cornelius Ryan must have cursed his bad luck. Below him the Allied armies were fighting for their first foothold on occupied European soil and he now risked missing his big 'scoop' because of a simple mechanical failure…

Dublin 1920

Ironically for a man who would become famous for writing about war, Cornelius Ryan was born into a city suffering the final stages of the Irish War of Independence. Dublin in the summer of 1920 was full of political tensions and that atmosphere often spilled over into family households.

Although Catholics, the six Ryan brothers of Emor Street had a long family tradition of service in the British army and were still loyal to their former employer. Cornelius would later joke that they had been 'tall guardsmen' but the Ryans were short in stature, with his father John Joseph (Jack or JJ to his family) suffering the added disadvantage of having chronic Asthma. He had only managed to follow his brothers into the army during World War One because medical examiners often overlooked minor illnesses in any Irishman willing to fight for 'King and Country'. Luckily he arrived in France only a few months before the conflict ended and was discharged with a full pension for a "war-related illness" he already had when he signed up in the first place!

Returning to Dublin, Jack married his childhood sweetheart Amelia (Emily) Clohisey from 33 Heytesbury Street in south Dublin. Although she had grown up on the next street up from Jack, her background was very different as her family was a recently returned émigré family that was more receptive to Irish nationalism. Emily herself had been a member of the quasi-military *Cumann na mBan* women's movement in her youth, whilst her brother John was long-rumoured to have been an intelligence man for the old IRA.

When Jack and Emily were married in 1919, her widowed father offered to sell the Clohisey family home to the young couple but with one condition – Jack allowed his father-in-law and his bachelor brother-in-law John to remain in the house with them. This odd set-up would lead to two opposing political traditions under the same roof, an awkward situation not helped by John Clohisey's habit of calling Jack Ryan 'George' to his face.

In total Emily and Jack were to have eight children – six of whom survived. By the 1930s there were five boys and one girl in the house: Cornelius, born in 1920; a second son Joseph in 1922; Gerard in 1928; daughter Kathleen in 1931; David in 1934; and John Junior in 1936.

Compared to many of the neighbouring areas near the city centre, their life was middle class and the Ryans were certainly well-off for their time. Jack Ryan had a secure job as a clerk at the Johnson Mooney & O'Brien bakery plus his British army pension. The couple owned their own home, had a motorbike with a side-car and even managed a family holiday for the children each year.

The only thing disrupting this comfortable situation was the strange political tension inside the home caused by having two father figures with wildly differing political views.

"We grew up believing everyone's uncle lived with the family and had as much power as your father," recalled younger brother David Ryan. "At the dinner table John and my father would be sparring off each other. It was light-hearted but there was an underlying background there. They would get under each other's skins but strangely the overall outcome of that, as children, we all had a very broad outlook on the world." [1] Cornelius would later write that he hovered between extremes, never knowing whether to 'knock the head off the nearest Britisher' or sing *God Save The King*. "I have often tried to analyse it, for I'm convinced that half of Ireland's troubles lie in this trait of studying the politics of two countries (England and Ireland) instead of concentrating on one – Ireland." [2]

Whilst his father largely kept a low profile, his one big chance to make a point appears to have been on Wednesdays when his wife cashed his British army pension.

"When mother gave him the British pension book to sign, my father would taunt her about the crown on the cover, playfully suggesting that she shouldn't have anything to do with the 'King's Shilling'," laughed Cornelius' brother Gerard Ryan. "He would say that 'Harps and Shamrocks' don't pay too much. It was friendly banter but he was also using it as his moment of glory." [3]

Thankfully the Ryan children grew up in a literate household, as their mother had trained as a teacher in the local Carmelite School. She was determined to pass on a respect for books to them and family legend has it that any writing talent Cornelius inherited came from her.

There had always been a link between the Clohiseys and the world of publishing. Although it is said Ryan's grandfather got into trouble for writing political pamphlets, this probably refers to his mother's uncle Malachy who ran a bookshop on Bedford Row at the turn of the 20th century. [4]

Whether an embellishment or a genuine mistake by his wife when she compiled his posthumous *A Private Battle* memoir, their stories were mixed up. Although his Ryan grandfather had been a compositor on *The Freeman's Journal* newspaper, he wasn't a journalist and certainly didn't end up in Mountjoy prison for his writings. This appears to have been an exaggeration of the fact that Malachy Clohisey had a small printing press in his bookshop, on which radical pamphlets might have been produced. Someone might have gone to prison for this but it certainly wasn't a Ryan or a Clohisey!

Unfortunately, this link between his mother's family and publishing came to an end in the first decade of the 20th century – mainly because Malachy Clohisey was fond of race horses and lost control of his bookshop. Now the only reminder is a mention of a "Clohissey's" bookshop in James Joyce's famous Dublin novel *Ulysses*.

Although they were only born two years apart, Cornelius' relationship with his younger brother Joseph appears to have suffered from the fact that whilst Cornelius was very much a Clohisey, Joseph Junior was definitely a Ryan. "Emily was a large woman, passing her genes onto Con who ended up being a large man," remembered Elizabeth 'Maisey' Ludlow, a next-door-neighbour and childhood friend. "Joseph took after the Ryans and was much smaller – something that lead to some bitterness between the two oldest brothers." [5]

Cornelius was much closer to his friend Freddie Ludlow from 34 Heytesbury Street during his childhood. He became like a brother after Freddie's own brother was killed in a motorbike accident in 1933. The two were the same age and became inseparable, often playing with the Darragh brothers from number 49. In those days motorcars were a rarity on Dublin's streets, so the boys often played football right outside on the road itself. "They were all very innocent boys really," recalled Maisey Ludlow. "They had a large wooden board which they used to set up in Con's dining room on which they would play table tennis. On Saturdays they used to take the board down to the Darragh's father's school opposite the children's hospital on Harcourt Street and play there."

Ryan family home, 1932

Cornelius' education was entrusted to the Christian Brothers, a Catholic school just around the corner on Synge Street. The school had a strong nationalist ethos, with games such as Gaelic football and hurling rather than soccer or rugby. 'The Brothers', as they were called, had a reputation for giving their students a good education but unfortunately this strict regime was often maintained using a teacher's fist or leather belt. [6]

His schooling might have been wasted if it hadn't been for English teacher Frank MacManus – a part-time novelist. Unlike the frustrated young religious staff, McManus was a more relaxed lay teacher in his forties whose status as a 'civilian' with a love of learning gained the respect and interest of his pupils. To help the students to discover literature for themselves, MacManus even encouraged Ryan's class to set up its own student magazine as a rival to the official *Our Boys*. This soon met with disapproval from the school authorities and another experiment in free-thinking was stifled – much to the disillusionment of the more independent pupils.

Ryan wasn't the only Synge Street boy to be inspired by MacManus to become a writer. One of his other classmates was James Kelly (only a month older than Ryan), who would later author the classic Dublin novel *Strumpet City* under his pen name of James Plunkett. Whether they were close friends at school is now lost to history but it is a fact that Plunkett followed his mentor MacManus into state broadcaster RTÉ as a radio producer in the 1950s – a career path Ryan himself would probably have taken if he had remained in Dublin. [7] Having left school before completing his Leaving Certificate, Ryan enrolled at the private secretarial college on Harcourt Street run by his friend Donnie Darragh's father. Alex Darragh had great connections in business and a good job was guaranteed for anyone who finished the course. [8]

As well as his academic horizons, Ryan's social life offered plenty of distractions at this time – much to the displeasure of his mother. Living within ten minutes walk of Dublin's fashionable St. Stephen's Green and Grafton Street, Ryan soon frequented many of the city's best pubs and cafes.

His coming of age also coincided with the growing influence of American popular culture and his circle of friends were heavily influenced by the music of Hollywood movies. They soon called themselves 'The Columbians' after the record label of their hero, singer Bing Crosby. His father Jack had always been musical and had encouraged his children to take up an instrument at an early age. Cornelius had been playing the violin since the age of seven and went to night courses at the Royal College of Music to improve his playing. He even formed the 'Hi-Lo Orchestra' band with his friends to perform at dance nights at a local tennis club but Ryan's mother put an end to this because she believed it was interfering with his college studies.

When he eventually completed his course, Ryan was placed in an English insurance firm on Dublin's Kildare Street, but the ongoing bitterness between the Dublin and London governments during the 1930s would mean it was short-lived. A tariff war between Éamon de Valera's government and London saw the Irish government introduce legislation limiting foreign ownership of insurance companies and Ryan's new employer was forced to close its Dublin office. [9] Thankfully, Alex Darragh came to the rescue again and secured a job at the recently opened Collinstown airport just north of the capital in 1939. Although the airport had been planned in the mid-1930s as a prestigious project to establish Ireland on the aerospace map, it was destined to open just as the clouds of war loomed and civilian aviation came to an abrupt halt. What at first seemed like a great opportunity for the young man soon turned into a frustrating and boring routine.

In his smart uniform, the 6-foot 2-inch young man cut a striking figure and was put in charge of escorting passengers to and from their plane. As passenger numbers were much lower than expected, no public transport was established for the new airport and Ryan was often forced to take the same Aer Lingus bus from O'Connell Street with the passengers. They were often shocked to see their 'pilot' carrying their bags to the airplane!

"He had a beautiful uniform and looked the part. With a big cap, brass buttons and all that kind of stuff. You would have imagined he was at least a captain," laughed Gerard Ryan. [10]

Unfortunately, only 5,000 passengers passed through the airport during its first year, and it was often closed at 7.30 pm when the final flight from Liverpool had landed. The only highlight for Ryan during this period was when he was photographed carrying the bags of Taoiseach Éamon de Valera – something his mother took great pride in.

In 1940, bored by the daily routine at the airport, Ryan drifted towards an amateur theatre group at the Father Matthew Hall on Church Street. Although he had no wish to become an actor, he hoped it might be an opportunity to write for the stage. However, the only writing Ryan was destined to do there was as an official note-taker for increasingly angry actor meetings. The theatre group was sponsored by the religious Capuchin Brothers order but its insistence that the actors attend a weekly temperance meeting meant the group's days were numbered. It was during this period that Ryan submitted several scripts to national broadcaster RTÉ for its 'Radio Reveals' programme, but these weren't accept. Luckily another escape route presented itself towards the end of 1940 when a regular visitor to Dublin airport, Canadian 'biscuit magnate' and Westminster MP Garfield Weston (who owned several bakeries in Ireland and was always on the lookout for new talent), offered the 20-year-old Ryan a trainee managerial position in London. Although the threat of the Blitz loomed large, Cornelius' main worry was his mother's reaction to him leaving a steady job and he had to ask Weston to make a personal visit to his home to reassure her that he would be safe in London. [11]

With his mother appeased, Ryan handed in his resignation at the airport on Christmas Eve 1940 and was spirited out of the house before she could change her mind.

Cornelius as a young man

London 1941

Although he would often inflate his connection to Garfield Weston MP, in reality Cornelius Ryan was only invited to London to take up the post of trainee manager at one of his factories in Battersea. With this in mind, Ryan was put to work distributing biscuits to Blitz victims but for someone with ambitions towards journalism, it must have been a fascinating introduction to the bombed-out city. Almost immediately, he realised being a factory manager was no more interesting than his old job at Dublin airport and he began submitting small news stories to various London press agencies.

"I wrote most nights, training myself, producing reams of stuff that embarrasses me now," he admitted later. [12]

But his perseverance worked and he was offered a 'copy boy' position by the Reuters news agency at its prestigious Fleet Street office. This must have been a dream come true for the 21-year-old, as he now found himself, literally, in the heart of most famous street for journalism in the world. He soon made his face known to the other hacks in the local pubs.

Sometime during 1943, Ryan encountered another recently arrived Fleet Street barfly, the famed American reporter Walter Cronkite. The two quickly became friends.

"He was the youngest fellow in the pub on the day I meet him, and he didn't get any older in the years that I knew him!" laughed Cronkite years later. "He was delightful from the beginning, if a little precocious. He was never one to remain silent when the conversation was lagging and could always bring it to life. We called him 'Corny' but wouldn't for a moment have wanted to silence him because he was a delight to be with. All the other reporters thought he exemplified the best of the Irish – a good story teller, a great guy at the bar." [13]

At that stage of the war though, most of the young reporters hanging around the bars of Fleet Street still didn't fully understand the realities of the war in Europe.

Thankfully, the routine was again broken for Ryan when he landed a full-time reporting job on the *Daily Telegraph* in 1943 and was assigned unofficial 'spying' missions during trips back home to see his family. Because the newspaper's existing reporter in Dublin was subject to Ireland's strict censorship laws, Ryan started smuggling information out about conditions in neutral Ireland. Eventually, when two embarrassing articles appeared in the *Telegraph* in March 1944 detailing sightings of a "German bomber" over Dublin (it was actually an off-course American plane) the Irish ambassador to London angrily approached newspaper owner Lord Camrose demanding to know who had written them. [14]

It wasn't long before Irish attention focused on Ryan as the 'itinerant correspondent' and a member of the Irish police named Gantly was tasked with cornering him on his next visit home. On questioning Ryan in April, the two men got on so well that the policeman's official report was less than incriminating. "He represents himself as a nationalistic Irishman whose private views could not permit him take a line of conduct prejudicial to the interests of this country," Gantly wrote.

When Defence Minister Frank Aiken read the report, he opined: "I haven't the slightest doubt that he is wrong in thinking Ryan is not the author of the reports in question. I have moreover, the word of the British Press attaché (in private conversation) for the fact that Ryan approached him for 'guidance' and seemed disinclined to take the advice he got to 'lay off'." [15]

Although Ireland's neutrality meant it should have been equally neutral to all countries involved in the conflict, Dublin was very much a 'neutral ally'. Although relations had suffered because of Churchill's personal bitterness towards De Valera, the Irish people were mostly on the side of the British and Americans.

Although Ireland had escaped the physical damage of the war, it was suffering economically. Basics such as meat, eggs and milk could be found in abundance but cooking fuel, flour, sugar, tea and cigarettes were hard to find.

The 'Battle of the Atlantic' had resulted in severe shortages of oil and coal, resulting in the closure of many Irish factories. Ironically, this was a boon to British industry, for tens of thousands of unemployed Irishmen headed to England in search of regular work. Many either enlisted in the military or found jobs in the struggling war industries, thereby creating a more positive image of the Irish in Britain.

In the run up to D-Day, Ryan wrote a lengthy article in the *Daily Telegraph* detailing how Ireland was suffering because of her neutrality.

"Now, more than at any other time in her history, Eire finds that she has to support herself nearly completely," wrote Ryan. "Despite the precautions taken by the Government in husbanding essentials, the position is rapidly becoming worse, and the Irishman knows that with the opening of the Allied offensive, goods which Eire might have received will be diverted to the Continent." [16]

Reporting such as this impressed his editors, and he was soon assigned to one of the biggest stories of the war – the imminent allied invasion of Europe. It is remarkable that a young man from a still suspect 'neutral ally' was being given access to one of the most closely guarded secrets of the war, just as the Allies were doing everything they could to isolate Ireland as a source of possible leaks. It was another sign of his growing reputation within the *Daily Telegraph.*

As only the top-tier reporters would get to see it all 'on the ground' right from the beginning, Ryan would have to be content with watching D-Day from an American B-26 Marauder bomber and was sent to a US Air Force base in the south of England to wait. Unfortunately, he hadn't been able to tell his parents and they were soon making enquires to the newspaper to see if anything serious had happened to their son. Their worries only grew when he failed to ring them on his 24th birthday on 5th June, so they were shocked and delighted to read his first D-Day reports two days later. [17]

D-Day 1944

In the early hours of 6th June 1944, Cornelius Ryan had been called into the airbase briefing room and told they were flying over Normandy later that morning to support the invasion of Europe. Although he was given the honour of accompanying the Commanding Officer in his own personal bomber, this turned out to be a mixed blessing because it was the only plane to develop a technical fault and had to return to base five miles short of its target. As they turned 180 degrees and flew back towards England one can only imagine Ryan's horror at the realisation that his long-awaited scoop was quickly disappearing. Thankfully, repairs to the plane only took a few hours and by the early afternoon they were over France once again. Ironically, this later trip over Normandy allowed Ryan to get a better view of the invasion's progress.

As they flew over the invasion beaches he was amazed at the spectacle below: "Away to the west I saw a sight I shall never forget. Hundreds of ships of every kind were moving towards France. From our height they were only distinguishable by the white wash which churned from their sterns. They looked as if they were strung together by some invisible chain.

"Suddenly below us I saw what appeared to be heavy cruisers. They followed each other in circles, and as each came abreast of the French coast it fired a broadside. As they fired their guns a black plume of flame rolled forward across the water for perhaps 30 or 40 yards. No sooner had the smoke disappeared from one cruiser than another was firing. We saw them firing as we went in to bomb our target. They were still firing relentlessly when we came out." [18]

Their main target was a German position several miles inland and although Ryan had been warned to expect enemy fighters, he was still relieved to note that the only aircraft in the air were allied ones. As they returned to base Ryan would have been furiously typing up his dispatch, aware that the earlier technical problems with the plane might have caused him to miss his deadline.

Ryan covered D-Day from a B-26 bomber

In fact, his observations were some of the most up-to-date to reach the newspaper and he made the front page of the next morning's edition.

Four days later he was once again over France in an American bomber, attacking a German gun battery on the Cherbourg peninsula. As flak shells burst around the Marauder, Ryan watched through the gunner's window.

"Through the plane I could get the strong scent of cordite fumes," he told *Telegraph* readers. "Still in formation and with wingtips so close that it seemed as if they might touch at any moment, we turned and headed inland. Ahead of me the bombs from the other formations spiralled downwards. They had found the target. A quick movement of the colonel's left-hand and our bombs had fallen. I saw the whole area of the target covered in a second with a mass of explosions. The concrete fort disintegrated and pieces of it flew up in the air. We had hit the target, and turning, we streaked for home." [19]

Two days later, he was on a hastily organised attack on a railway marshalling yard on the outskirts of Rennes. Ryan's plane came under heavy flak shelling again.

"Tiny fragments of shrapnel rattled all along the plane's fuselage. After every burst the concussion vibrated the whole plane. Then something hit the armoured plate beneath me and a wisp of black smoke curled into the waist-gun aperture. The blow was so severe that particles of dirt and cartridge cases lying on the floor of the plane were thrown up." [20]

But once again they hit their target and headed home. As the reporter filed his story to London, the B-26 was refuelled and its crew flew off on their next mission.

Ryan's next flight was on 13th June, when they destroyed German tanks hiding in the forests during the Battle for Villers Bocage. Ryan watched in amazement as bombs ripped up the roadway in front of two tanks, leaving them stranded to be finished off by the next plane in the formation. [21]

Despite their near total domination of the skies over northern France, the Allies were surprised by the appearance of the unmanned V-1 'flying bomb' – a new Nazi wonder weapon. Tuesday 20th June saw Ryan taking part in a massive 3,000 bomber-strong formation targeting the V-1 launch sites, but these were very difficult to spot from the air. Even when flying directly above a V-1 site in the Pas de Calais it was almost invisible to the untrained eye.

"At first in our search we passed right over it without knowing," wrote Ryan. "It lay at the intersection of a crossroads and the actual launching platform was practically invisible from the air because it ran along the road, its white concrete structure merging with the colour of the roadway.

"Through binoculars the platform appeared to be a long, shallow affair, about 200 feet long and 25 feet wide, rising steeply at one end. From our height, it was a mere pinpoint and on measuring it I found it to be about the length of the point of my pencil."

Bizarrely the Germans were afraid to fire on the allied aircraft above, lest they reveal the location of the still top-secret launch sites. This tactic backfired because it allowed the Marauder crew to rehearse their bombing run in peace for 40 minutes before they eventually destroyed the launcher. Then as they turned for home, Ryan spotted one of the pilotless weapons below them, making its own way to England.

On 22nd June the reporter witnessed the aerial bombardment of the port of Cherbourg. When their plane was over the southern suburbs, the pilot suddenly told his passenger that they had a "runaway propeller" – one of the engine's aerofoils was revolving much faster than normal and risked tearing the plane apart. Just at that moment flak fire opened up on them.

"Fragments ripped along the bottom of the plane with a harsh noise and the concussion tossed the plane about like a cork," Ryan wrote. "Then a glass panel directly in front of me in the nose was shattered by a piece of shrapnel. We turned and with the port propeller moving so fast that the whole engine nacelle vibrated, we left the French coast and headed for the Channel. The vibration became worse and our pilot signalled to the other members of the formation that we were in distress. But with great coaxing by the pilot and co-pilot our plane reached the base and safety." [22]

Perhaps thankful that his time at the airbase was finally coming to an end, Ryan flew his last mission on Sunday 25th June. This targeted the railway marshalling yard near Chartres and turned out to be a relatively uneventful affair – the only highlight being a sighting of the river Seine from the cockpit window. [23]

The young reporter was extremely grateful to his US Air Force hosts. Not only had they kept him alive during eleven bombing missions over France but they had helped him earn a solid reputation back at the *Daily Telegraph*.

France 1944

Ryan probably knew what was ahead of him when the *Daily Telegraph*'s Lord Camrose invited him into his top-floor office on Fleet Street for a chat. The proprietor told the young Irishman that he was being assigned to General George Patton's Third Army as it prepared to depart for France but he felt he was being picked because his nationality made him expendable, rather than for any particular affinity the Irish had with Americans. [24]

By this stage of the war the younger second-tier reporters had grown frustrated at being left behind, so this new assignment was a welcome break for the rising war correspondent. It must have been a relief when Ryan arrived in Southampton and attached a Third Army shoulder patch to his Saville Row-tailored uniform. [25]

The assembled war correspondents preparing to go into Europe were in a strange limbo – having been granted 'quasi-officer' status to guarantee better treatment by the Germans in the event of being captured, they were nevertheless viewed with suspicion by the military. In France, there was a constant battle with their handlers as the reporters demanded ready access to jeeps and drivers. [26]

Unfortunately for Ryan, his first experience of battle on the ground was quite embarrassing but he was able to laugh about it with family later.

"The first time he came under fire he jumped for the first foxhole," is how his brother Gerard Ryan recalled the incident. "As explosions boomed around him, he suddenly heard a voice saying 'Can I help you, Sir?' It was a big 6-foot 4-inch Negro GI festooned with grenades, who pulled him out of the foxhole. I can't say he was too proud of that but he still told the story!" [27]

The Irishman also drew attention to himself in other ways, often being treated with suspicion by US military policemen who were convinced his accent made him the world's worst German spy. [28]

But after he had learned the GI basics (such as eating with the fork in his right hand) he fit in and soon found his natural home: "Amongst those brash, irreverent, confident soldiers, I found my spiritual home and, covering the war in Europe, I furthered my training as a reporter by working with some of the finest correspondents the United States had...Young, dumb, brash, and Irish, I learned more from them than any school could ever have taught me." [29]

Throughout this time, Ryan was also able to keep in contact with his family in Ireland, with occasional calls to the only person on Heytesbury Street who had a telephone – the local dentist.

"There was only one telephone on our street, at Jack Carey's surgery," recalled David Ryan. "One of his children would come charging down the street to tell my mother that Con was on the phone. She would go charging up the street, no matter what she was wearing, because he only had X amount of minutes to talk." [30]

Whilst his son reported on Patton's progress across Europe his proud father kept a scrapbook of all his articles, as well as pinning small flags onto a wall map to show the younger Ryan children where their glamorous brother was.

His brother David doesn't think Cornelius developed any personal hatred of Germans during the war: "He just saw people for what they were and I don't think he attributed blame to the individual soldier – Tommy, Jerry or Yank."

Ryan even showed a certain sympathy to the plight of the retreating German troops.

"Driving along a road in this sector of the front today, I came upon a scene of the worst carnage I have seen yet in France," wrote Ryan on 2nd August 1944. "Along both sides of the road lay the twisted wreckage of a complete German armoured column. It had been trapped, bumper to bumper, and blown to pieces. To walk down this road we had to squeeze our way between the packed vehicles and step over the German dead."

"Bewildered German troops are wandering through woods and forests and are being rounded up. These German infantrymen, left behind to fight some sort of rear-guard action, are being found at every turn. They are completely dazed and confused." [31]

The chaotic retreat of the German army was confirmed a few days later when a group of them actually surrendered to a group of war reporters, including Ryan, who had just arrived in the medieval harbour town of Mont St. Michel. As their military driver was the only one with a gun on him, he locked the Germans up in the local prison and the correspondents then proceeded to have lunch with the town's mayor. [32]

As the German presence in western France collapsed, the attention of the correspondents turned to the imminent liberation of Paris.

On the morning of Friday 18th August, Ryan instructed his driver to head in the direction of Paris. When only 40 miles from the city he managed to talk his way onto a small Piper Cub spotter plane and later wrote about seeing roads "black with allied columns" heading towards the city. [33]

As the liberation of Paris neared, relations between the various factions of the press pack deteriorated as they grew suspicious of each other's 'Paris scoop'. This tense situation reached fever pitch when the correspondents reached their new base camp only 20 miles from the French capital.

Most of this ill-feeling came from those who had been in France since D-Day, as they believed the second wave of newcomers didn't deserve to be interfering with their hard-won exclusive. This situation wasn't helped by a lack of space at the press camp, with time served in France being no guarantee of a warm bed for the night.

Walter Cronkite remembered that the reporters had to share military jeeps together as they made their way into the newly liberated French capital. He recalled that Ryan ended up in the same vehicle as Andy Tully of the *Boston Traveler*, one of the 'veterans' who had covered the allied campaign since D-Day.

"They were coming into Paris and came across Clichy Street. Tully, who often pulled his leg quite a bit, turned to Connie and said 'We are passing Cliché, say something'!" [34]

The liberation of Paris was everything they could have wished for, and as five hundred excited correspondents headed for the Hotel Scribe, their unofficial 'press club', world-weary reporter Ernie Pyle famously quipped "anybody who doesn't sleep with a woman tonight is just an exhibitionist." [35]

"The Scribe hotel bar promptly became the scene of the greatest party of all time," wrote reporter Iris Carpenter, a rare female in the macho press pack. "Champagne corks popped with the monotony of a machine-gun barrage. Every few minutes somebody would come in from some far distant front. Never mind whether they had any right to cover the story or not, this was the Paris Party and everyone in war correspondents' uniform was determined to be in on it." [36]

At the Scribe, Ryan was delighted to meet the American writer Ernest Hemingway as he held court in the hotel bar, but this interlude to the war could not last and all too soon Ryan was back reporting on the Third Army.

Reporting on Patton's race towards the industrial heartland of Germany, Ryan was soon quoting the general as saying that he expected to be "knocking on the gates of Germany within a week." [37]

Years later, Ryan would write that at one of his daily press conferences Patton told the assembled press corps that "maybe there are 5,000, maybe 10,000 Nazi bastards in their concrete foxholes before the Third Army. Now, if Ike stops holding Monty's hand and gives me the supplies, I'll go through the Siegfried Line like shit through a goose." [38]

As he told them this he was standing in front of a large map which was illuminated by lights placed inside up-turned German army helmets! [39]

On 14th September, Ryan reported on the 'fall' of the deserted Maginot Line and spent three hours inside the infamous French underground complex guided by a local French youth who had helped keep it in working order for the Germans, even though it had proved to be militarily useless during the 1940 invasion of France. Entering a concealed doorway on the edge of a forest, Ryan descended a spiral staircase: "In murky, damp darkness 100 feet below the level of the earth in the electrical power house I watched as he pressed the starter button of the huge Diesel engine. The Maginot Line had come to life again. The Germans did not demolish or mine the vast network of tunnels and underground fortifications. Even the guns were still oiled and in working condition." [40]

On-the-spot reports like these were what being a frontline reporter was all about for Ryan, but it often involved long drives through a series of checkpoints to make a deadline.

By the time the weary frontline reporter arrived back at the press camp to file his dispatch, he would often discover he had been scooped by colleagues who had remained in the bar and written articles using information culled from the official daily communiqué. This was disparagingly referred to as 'magic carpeting' by the braver frontline reporters and was greatly exacerbated when these lazy hacks spiced-up their articles using gossip overheard in the bar.

One day a frustrated Ryan saw his opportunity for revenge and nearly caused an international incident. In September, upon returning with news of the allied capture of the French city of Nancy, he noticed an English reporter listening in. Ryan then added the startling (but ridiculous) claim that the Germans had counterattacked using a new squadron of women tank drivers. Unfortunately, the English hack included the information in his dispatch, something that shocked the American censor who checked his copy. Although the US military was relieved to find this was an internal Fleet Street affair, the Englishman's editor was still informed and the lazy hack was recalled to London. [41]

By the end of the month, Ryan finally caught up with the V-1 flying bomb when he inspected one of its secret underground factories located in an old French iron mine. It had only been days from full-production and the Irishman reminded his *Daily Telegraph* readers that it could have manufactured five hundred missiles per day. [42]

Despite signs that the Germans were struggling, it was obvious that the pace of the allied thrust was slowing down and in November the ancient fortified French city of Metz, a few miles from the German border, became a key psychological objective for both sides. This resulted in a long drawn-out battle that became known as the Siege of Metz. [43]

On 25th November Patton drove into Metz the conquering hero but even the flamboyant general was worried that the war was growing "stale and sluggish". [44]

As the weather grew ever worse and the Third Army fought through the mud, the ordinary Wehrmacht soldiers were replaced by hardened SS men more willing to hold the line whilst the poorer quality troops fell back into Germany to fight another day.

That December, Adolf Hitler made his final gamble of the war with a counter-offensive through the Ardennes forest which became infamous as the Battle of the Bulge. As Field Marshall Gerd Von Rundstedt's troops smashed through inexperienced American divisions in a bold attempt to capture the port of Antwerp and isolate the Allied forces to the north, the Third Army was forced to make an unexpected sharp turn northwards to help. [45]

As war reporters watched C-47 Dakota aircraft dropping supplies on the besieged American garrison in Bastogne, it appeared a lost cause to them. When the 101st Airborne Division's General Maxwell Taylor approached four correspondents (including Ryan and Walter Cronkite) huddled around a camp fire, Ryan spoke for all of them when he said there were "no volunteers" for the general's offer of a ride into Bastogne.

Unfortunately the reporters missed a big scoop as the General managed to slip past German lines and was drinking cognac with his men that very evening! [46]

Germany 1945

After Hitler's final failed offensive, the Third Army resumed its advance through two feet of snow towards the German border. [47]

Resistance was collapsing, and when Ryan entered the town of Trier it was practically deserted. What remained of the city centre was eerily covered in white towels draped from windows by long-gone civilians. This surreal scene was compounded when Ryan watched a single German soldier calmly climb into a US jeep in front of him and surrender.

In a long article published on 14th March 1944 Ryan wrote about how he now believed the Germans had finally lost the "taste for war" but were still not used to the fact that they were on the losing side.

"They know that they cannot expect help from their conquerors, though some of the more courageous try to win over American soldiers by being friendly. Some of these beg for lifts in passing jeeps or trucks, offering schnapps or some other gifts. They smile and those that speak English will invariably tell you that they hate Hitler and that it was all a terrible mistake.

"When the American soldiers refuse to converse with them or accept their proffered gifts, and abruptly tell them to keep moving, their attitude changes. Then Americans are not 'gentlemen' any more, they are 'evil people'."

"Though the American soldier is a very good-natured and good-humoured individual, I find that he is intensely bitter towards German civilians and wants to have nothing to do with them." [48]

On 8th April, Patton's troops overran a prisoner-of-war camp at Ohrdruf, near the Thuringian Forest. Although it had mainly been used for eastern European prisoners, a few downed US airmen had been kept there too. The arriving Americans were deeply shocked to find evidence of war crimes, with many of the prisoners murdered by the SS just before the liberation. "The partly clad bodies of 31 men were huddled grotesquely together where they had been killed by

SS guards because they were too ill to be moved," wrote Ryan. "Shot in the back of the head, with the exception of one American, who had been shot in the throat."

Feelings were naturally running high, and when Third Army troops had heard enough of local denials about knowledge of what had gone on at the camp, prominent citizens were forced to tour it to see for themselves.

Ryan reported their military guide shouting: "Now you know why we will never be your friends; why we will always hate you; why we will always be enemies." [49]

Patton with war correspondents including Ryan

With the war in Europe at an end, the only two correspondents who had accompanied the Third Army right from the beginning in Normandy, Ryan and Robert Cromie of *The Chicago Tribune*, went to say their goodbyes to its eccentric general in his personal trailer and were surprised to see him reading a book about Napoleon. Before letting them leave, Patton warned the two young men of the growing menace of the Red Army and opined that he thought the Soviets had played the western allies for "suckers". [50]

"Con regarded Patton for what he was - 'Blood and Guts' - and I think he also firmly believed that Patton was done away with by his own troops because he was hated by the ordinary soldier," recalled his brother David Ryan. "There was a strong opinion around that time that Patton had been killed by a landmine planted by his own men, and that opinion was expressed by Con. It wasn't an accident and Patton eventually got his comeuppance." [51]

With his time in Europe coming to an end, there was a chance that he might see some of the still-raging Pacific war and he returned to London in time for the *Daily Telegraph* to reassigned him to the Far East.

Ryan took the opportunity to visit his family in Dublin, whom he hadn't seen for nearly a year and surprised them by presenting them with a loaf of white bread from London – a rarity in Dublin at that moment. The war-weary reporter took a quiet stroll along the streets of Dublin with his 17-year-old brother Gerard and it wasn't long before the exotic sight of a 6-foot 2-inch man in US Army uniform attracted unwanted attention.

"Yanks in full uniform were a rarity at the time," remembered Gerard. "Con was walking down O'Connell Street when a man approached offering directions to the 'American visitor'. Pretty soon Con realised this man was also trying to pick his pocket! With that he picked the man up and threw him head first onto the road." [52]

Japan 1945-46

Ryan set off on the long journey to the Pacific theatre of war via New York, sailing the Atlantic on the Queen Mary with returning American soldiers. He arrived in Tokyo just in time to witness the Japanese surrender aboard the *USS Missouri*. The next few weeks were something of an anti-climax, as he reported on his largely futile attempts to track down a mysterious secret society called the 'Black Dragons' who were rumoured to run the country. His researches came to nothing and anyone he cornered who was thought to be involved always, naturally, denied involvement.

A real story eventually presented itself when a group of press accompanied the US military when it went to arrest former war-time leader General Hideki Tojo. By then, the general was so despised by his own side for losing the war that he hadn't been able to entice any of his former colleagues to participate in a traditional 'hara-kiri' suicide ceremony. Now, as he saw the Americans arriving at his door he simply took a revolver and fired a shot into his own chest. The bullet missed his heart and the press pack was treated to the sight of the bleeding general, fully conscious, sitting in his chair waiting for death. [53]

"The whole thing was a cross between a Marx brothers' movie and an Irish wake," is how Ryan described the bizarre spectacle. "Tojo leaned back and a long squirt of blood shot out of his chest like water coming out under pressure from a hole in a burst pipe. A large pool of blood was slowly gathering on the floor. Tojo groaned, clenched and unclenched his hands in spasms of agony." [54]

Forty minutes after he tried to kill himself, the bored reporters moved the barely alive general, but this intervention (which was doubtless their attempt to quicken history) saved his life because the blood he has been suffocating on emptied out of the hole in his chest. Almost immediately Tojo began to revive, much to the chagrin of the four correspondents who had moved him.

American doctors later estimated that five more minutes of patience would have been rewarded by the correspondents having the pleasure of writing Tojo's obituary.

Apart from this bizarre incident, Ryan's time in Japan was remarkably uneventful because the press was largely prevented by General Douglas MacArthur's censor from filing any controversial stories. Censorship had officially ended in October 1945, but MacArthur's staff was accustomed to controlling his image and it wasn't long before members of the press were at war with his headquarters.

They took a particular dislike to Brigadier General LeGrande A. Diller, the head of MacArthur's PR. His 'Killer Diller' nickname was given for his fondness for destroying copy with his censor's pen. Since both groups were squeezed into the Dai-Iti Hotel, it was decided to establish a 'Tokyo Correspondents' Association' elsewhere to try gain some independence. Their five-story hostel would be open to any journalist visiting Japan. [55]

It took a team of fifty Japanese workers under the supervision of the US military nearly two weeks to clean up the mess. After a month the building was nearing completion, with new beds flown in from the Philippines for the correspondents. An advert was placed in the local newspaper asking for kitchen staff and over 2,000 turned up. When the crowd broke through the door several times, Ryan helped the cook interview hundreds of people for the prized kitchen positions. Many were so desperate for work that they offered to work for free, if they could eat at the press club. Seventy locals were given jobs, but it was soon observed that this number had swelled to over one hundred. A careful check showed relations of many of the hired staff had found themselves 'jobs' within the building too. [56]

A more challenging task was creating a group of presentable waitresses to staff the club's meal tables. A bunch of the most promising contenders were groomed for the job.

"These girls, all about sixteen to twenty, were tired-looking, shabby little creatures who needed help, for most of them had suffered greatly during the war," observed Ryan.

It took the intervention of an American woman nurse to "restore the femininity these nervous creatures had once possessed." Parachute silk was fashioned into outfits and the girls were encouraged to bathe twice a day until they were clean. Lipstick, manicured nails and new stockings added to the transformation. After a week of regular bathing the waitresses became new people.

Soon the reporters were calling in 'favours' from various Army and Navy units. Even the Red Cross sent over a record player and over one hundred discs for the club's mess.

The two Japanese barmen were nicknamed 'Smithy' and 'Jackson' and had an ample supply of alcohol thanks to the quick-thinking of American correspondent Thomas Shafer. On hearing that one of the naval units that he was friendly with was returning to the US, he bought up their remaining supply of alcohol before the ship left harbour. This booty filled two trucks in total. [57]

When it was ready, the press corps cleared out their belongings at the Dai-Iti Hotel en masse and moved into 'No.1 Shimbun Alley'. Its official opening was marred by the fact that MacArthur turned down an invitation to attend but it soon became the 'in place' in Tokyo.

The Correspondents' Association delighted in reminding the staff of MacArthur's headquarters that they weren't welcome unless they were guests of a correspondent.

The early days in the Press Club were carefree, with many treating the club as their own bachelor pad. Most reporters shared rooms with four or five others, but a certain free-for-all atmosphere prevailed when it came to finding somewhere to sleep at the end of the day. Residents could never be sure that their bed would be free when they retired to their room.

While in Japan, Ryan visited Hiroshima and Nagasaki and considered the morality of the atomic bombs. As he wrote in the co-authored *The Star-Spangled Mikado*: "At least 90 percent of the correspondents felt it should not have been dropped, and everybody who visited the two places and saw the unimaginable destruction by the atomic bomb, knew a perfect blueprint for the plan of mankind's destruction had been completed...A visit to Hiroshima or Nagasaki convinces one the atomic bomb far transcends all other problems in the world today. There is not time to delay…the atomic race is in full swing."

In early summer 1946, dozens of the world's press spent several weeks aboard the *USS Appalachian* as it sailed for Bikini Atoll in the Marshall Islands in the Pacific. Their boredom was eased by the copious amounts of alcohol available and the knowledge that they were on their way to see a real-life nuclear explosion.

Up until that moment, only three atomic bombs had been exploded in total – the first at the Trinity test site in America and the other two on Hiroshima and Nagasaki – so 'the bomb' created an almost boyish excitement amongst war-hardened hacks who reckoned they had seen it all. To parade their nuclear monopoly with Operation Crossroads, the US ensured journalists from all over the world would be in attendance – including one from Russia! Although Ryan had seen the after-effects of the weapon in Japan, like most he was eager to see the raw power of the atom in action. [58]

The first 'A-Day' was scheduled for 1st July, with an air-dropped bomb detonating 500 feet above a fleet of 95 ships, including decommissioned US Navy vessels and captured German and Japanese warships. The bomb caused less damage than expected because it missed its aim point by 2,000 feet.

It was a great disappointment for the assembled press, owing to the fact that their observation ship was stationed too far away and the flash of the explosion was completely masked by the heavy welding glasses that they had been issued with. Astonishingly, even the sound of the explosion failed to reach them.

However, the second test on 25th July was everything they could have expected of an atomic explosion. This bomb was detonated in the sea at a depth of ninety feet, creating a giant wave that engulfed the target ships in millions of tonnes of water as it was thrown high into the air by the blast. It was one of the most iconic sights of the Atomic Age.

"The roar of the explosion lasted about 30 seconds, and ships in the observer fleet shuddered," enthused Ryan. "The column of water flung up reached 5,000 feet and had an estimated diameter of over 2,000 feet at the base. A blinding flash accompanied the explosion. Most of the observers were awed by the sight." [59]

Reporting the atomic tests on radio

USA 1947-49

Ryan's next assignment for the *Daily Telegraph* was to report on the end of the British mandate in Palestine. Jewish refugees were arriving daily on overcrowded ships and the British were refusing to let them land – even though many of the vessel's engines had been deliberately wrecked so that they could not be sent back to Europe. Some refugees even jumped into the sea, yelling "Death or Palestine" when British navy ships approached. [60]

Like many who knew of the plight of the Jews at the hands of the Nazis, Ryan had sympathy for the refugees and even felt that the British soldiers were acting like the "Black and Tans" back in Ireland. [61]

Over the next month, over 3,850 refugees were detained on impounded vessels at Tel Aviv. On one visit, Ryan described the appalling conditions they had to endure as they waited to be unloaded by the British authorities who didn't know what to do with them.

"When I climbed aboard the vessels this afternoon the decks and holds were crammed with thousands of tin cans of American and Italian rations which probably came from camps. The holds swarmed with people and one could not help but feel great pity for the children and babies," he wrote in the *Daily Telegraph*. [62]

During this period, Ryan also acted as a 'stringer' for the American press and had been supplied with a camera by *LIFE* magazine. When he used it to take a quick snap of a young Polish refugee girl and her brother he found himself in the middle of an emotional political issue.

"As I watched I saw a small girl of about ten, her eyes filled with tears, slowly make her way down the gangplank. In front of her was her baby brother with a filthy old blanket around his shoulders. The little girl had her arms around her brother and as I watched this shocking spectacle I realised that if I could capture these two children in a picture it would sum up the whole tragedy of Israel. Somehow I composed the picture fast and snapped the shutter. There wasn't time for a second shot, so I prayed that I had been right the first time."

It had been a lucky shot and it delighted the editors of *LIFE*, who then made it their 'Picture of the Week'. Ryan was later surprised to hear that the United Jewish Welfare Fund asked to use the image for its 1947 poster campaign entitled 'They Must Live!' and was equally shocked to be paid £650 in picture rights.

Bizarrely the photograph would 'come alive' again the following year when it was used in the Hollywood movie *The Boy with the Green Hair*. In this anti-war drama, the two refugees literally came out of the photograph and talked to the boy of the title. An attempt by the *Reader's Digest* in the 1970s to discover the identities of the two children was unsuccessful, but in 1984 *LIFE* selected the photograph as one of its 1,500 best images. [63]

Ever since Ryan's first contact with the Americans during the war he had wanted to move to the USA. It finally happened during a trip to New York in 1947 when he was offered a job on the international desk of Henry Luce's publishing empire – home of *LIFE* and *Time*. "To my amazement, the very day I reported in they asked me to go to the Dominican Republic – a place that, up to that time, I had never heard of," he admitted years later. Ryan spent the next several months on the Caribbean island not only researching the brutal Trujillo dictatorship but also trying to obtain a valid immigration visa to return to the US permanently. But ultimately he wasn't happy with his new employer: "I liked writing for *LIFE* but frankly I could not stand *Time*. Every week we were expected to climb into the 'Lucian' pulpit and remake the world." [64]

At the same time he was co-operating with his old Tokyo friend, the *New York Herald Tribune*'s Frank Kelley, to turn their old dispatches into the first book on the American occupation entitled *Star Spangled Mikado*. Perhaps to keep his options open further Ryan also invested some of his own money in a small literary journal called '*48 – The Magazine of the Year*'. This small 'digest' magazine was aimed at the large number of ex-soldiers who were then being educated thanks to the post-war 'GI Bill'. It was packed with political features, short works of fiction, and daring photography. It was owned by those who contributed and Ryan bought his way in as an 'assistant publisher' from the June 1948 issue but unfortunately it folded shortly afterwards. Sometime during 1949 the restless writer also joined a new special projects division of *Newsweek*, which saw him producing an early experiment in weekly television news broadcasting.

On a personal level, things were going well for Ryan as he had started dating a young American writer named Kathryn Morgan. Five years his junior, she came from a modest background and was the only child of the local postmaster of Oskaloosa in Iowa. Like Ryan, she had worked her way up, studying at the University of Missouri's School of Journalism before landing a job on *House & Garden* magazine in New York. They married in 1949 and used a Pan Am organised all-expenses-paid fifth-anniversary D-Day trip as their honeymoon. The young couple even stopped off in Dublin to see his family.

New Frontiers – 1950s

In 1950 Cornelius Ryan not only became an American citizen but also landed a full-time writing job on the popular weekly magazine *Collier's*.

Editors at the magazine had previously published an article by Ryan based on his biography of Douglas MacArthur, which had been put together with Frank Kelley to capitalise on the general's starring role in the Korean War. They were sufficiently impressed to hire him as an associate editor in early 1951.

To formally introduce their new Irish writer, the magazine offered him a prestigious cover story on modern Ireland to coincide with its 17th March St. Patrick's Day issue. The article turned out to be unlike anything that most Americans had read before, because it eschewed the standard clichés and presented a portrait of a young nation emerging as one of the modern post-Marshall Plan economies of Europe.

To old-school Irish-Americans, Ryan's take on Ireland was provocative because it presented a less than flattering view of Éamon de Valera's outgoing government. Drawing on interviews Ryan had conducted on his honeymoon trip to Dublin in 1949, the article praised the new coalition lead by Fine Gael's Liam Costello, and even included quotes from progressive liberal thinkers such as Sean MacBride and Noel Browne.

"They have brought cold realism to bear on Ireland's problems," wrote Ryan. "It is the direct antithesis of De Valera's mysticism, [who] showed the Irish the glories of the past. Costello is showing them the glories of the future.

"Without hatred or bitterness the Irish have been running their green isle as smoothly as an American corporation," he continued. "Rebuilding, revitalizing, and modernising ancient agricultural Ireland with hard-boiled realism instead of wild-eyed nationalism."

Ryan also attacked the "stage-Irish" who dominated American thinking on Ireland at the time: "As usual the American 'stage-Irish,' most of whom have never set foot in

Ireland anyway, but who seem bent on making Ireland, its government and its people appear irresponsible, undignified, contentious and farcical in the eyes of the Unites States, know precisely nothing of the facts."

Predictably, within days of the article appearing an organisation calling itself the 'United Irish Counties Association of New York' dismissed it as "inspired by the British Propaganda Bureau for the purpose of influencing American public opinion, lest in the future the Irish people should decide to take more vigorous action to end the partition of their country."

Spokesman Matthew Higgins was quoted in de Valera's Dublin-based *Irish Press* newspaper complaining that if *Collier's* had really been interested in the Republic of Ireland "it would have been good sense to engage a writer who was not so strongly steeped in British tradition as Mr. Ryan admittedly is." [65]

In this atmosphere, his cousin John Ryan wasn't too surprised to be approached by a friend in a pub off Grafton Street and half-jokingly told that "if that cousin of yours ever comes back he is going to be shot." [66]

Back in New York, Ryan was now busy working on another controversial Collier's project. Even now, looking back with hindsight, the fact that a mainstream publication could set out to show how the West could win a nuclear war at the height of the Cold War seems bizarre.

Although published at Halloween, this *Collier's* 'Preview of The War We Do Not Want' special issue was published without any intended dark-humour. As if to emphasis the point, its cover depicted a blue-helmeted United Nations' soldier in front of a map of Eastern Europe. Inside, the editorial thundered: "Alarmed at the creeping pessimism of the free world as it faced the threat of an unending series of Koreas, *Collier's* planned an unprecedented project…to demonstrate that if The War We Do Not Want is forced upon us, we will win." [67]

Since January of 1951, Ryan had been tasked with assembling the parts of this special issue, as it grew out of an idea he had originally pitched on how America would respond if it were attacked by the Soviet Union. The magazine's publisher Edward Anthony liked the idea so much that he commissioned an entire issue on the subject. [68]

To add to its shock value, the scale of the project was kept secret from most within the magazine, with only a handful of staff in-the-know. Ryan secretly contacted over twenty contributors, including broadcaster Edward R. Murrow, *Hiroshima* writer John Hersey, and author J. B. Priestly. Many of the contributors would later insist that they were unaware of the overall tone of 'Operation Eggnog', a fictional war that would see Washington, Chicago, Philadelphia, New York, London and Moscow all destroyed by nuclear bombs.

A sign of the importance given to this World War III special was the additional $40,000 spent on articles and artwork. When a total of nearly 4 million copies hit the newsstands, the public was largely horrified by the content. Artist Chesley Bonestell's photo-realistic paintings of atomic mushroom clouds over familiar landmarks in Manhattan and Washington didn't help. *Time* magazine called it "Armageddon in a full, fat 130-pages." [69]

Soon the contributors were called on to answer for their involvement. Murrow, inundated with angry letters from his radio audience, gave up trying to reply and simply threw them in a folder marked "*Collier's*/no answer/there isn't one!" [70] Other contributors were more supportive of the magazine.

Writing in the liberal New York publication *The Nation*, Walter Reuther wrote: "The failure to achieve what I believe would have been a worthy purpose was due in part to the terrifying and horrible scenes depicted in the art work. I believe the editors of *Collier's* had the best of intentions, and certainly it was my intention to contribute to the cause of world peace by participating. I believe, however, that the issue fails of that objective and I sincerely regret that it does." [71]

Almost immediately, Ryan was thrown into his next 'special project' to convince the American public that space travel was the next big thing – six years before Sputnik. This optimistic vision of the future was a direct consequence of the public's bad reaction to the World War III issue. Ironically, this gave ex-German rocket designer Wernher Von Braun the chance to pitch his grand vision of a space programme, harboured since he set out to develop the V-2 missile for the Nazis, directly to the American public. [72]

Gordon Manning, *Collier's* managing editor, focused on the German rocket scientist after hearing about him during a conference at the Hayden Planetarium in New York in October 1951. He saw the potential of it all as a more positive campaigning story and told Ryan to give it the 'Operation Eggnog' treatment.

To start his assignment, Cornelius Ryan travelled to a three-day space medicine conference in Texas that November, where the arrival of a writer from such a popular weekly magazine turned out to be a godsend to Von Braun, who was slowly growing frustrated at what he saw as America's continued disinterest in spaceflight. This was illustrated by the fact that his first non-fiction space book in English had just been rejected by seventeen publishers. Over the next several days, Von Braun and his 'inner circle' of followers pitched the idea of spaceflight to the captive reporter. Over dinner scientists Joseph Kaplan and Fred Whipple convinced the sceptical reporter that manned spaceflight was feasible in the near future. [73]

Once he was convinced that Von Braun's vision was sound, Ryan put all his writing skills into making spaceflight believable to the readers of *Collier's* magazine. In effect, and despite some scepticism from his own colleagues in the magazine's editorial office, he was adding credibility to the topic.

Back in New York, Ryan quickly arranged for all the principal participants to hold another private meeting at *Collier's* to get to work on the material for the magazine. The final list of contributors would include scientists Von Braun, Heinz Haber, Joseph Kaplan, Fred Whipple and space historian Willy Ley. Each expert was commissioned to submit a paper on his particular speciality, which would then be re-written by Ryan and Willy Ley to make it more readable to the general public.

Although Ryan had the full support of his immediate superior Gordon Manning from the start, the attitude of many others within the magazine often embarrassed him. Publisher Paul Smith called it all the "space cadet stuff". Outgoing editor Louis Ruppel, who had commissioned the World War III issue, made his own views of the Germans known when he approached Heinz Haber, pointed to his leather jacket and enquired if it was made of human skin!

The engineering designs sent by Von Braun in Texas to Ryan in New York were copied to Bonestell in California. Once the artists had finished their portrayal of Von Braun's designs, copies of these paintings were sent back to Von Braun for his approval. Although a slow process, the results were technically accurate illustrations that still stand up to this day. The artists even had time for visual jokes, and in the painting of the large space station sharp-eyed readers can find portrayals of Von Braun, Haber and Ley floating around inside. Ryan is even shown sitting inside the space station reading a copy of *Collier's* magazine. [74]

The association between these dreams of spaceflight and the realities of military rockets saw Ryan take the finished manuscripts to the Department of Defense in Washington for security clearance, because Von Braun and fellow German Heinz Haber were both employees of the US military and did not want to get in trouble with their employer for revealing sensitive military subjects.

The space special issue was published on 22nd March 1952, with its 15-page cover feature 'Man Will Conquer Space Soon!' accompanied by photo-realistic paintings of rockets, manned space shuttles and an orbiting space station. Although it still contained the Cold War paranoia of the era by warning readers (correctly as it turned out) that if the US didn't get into orbit first the Soviets would, it was a revelation to the readership. For the first time spaceflight was being given a direct pitch to the US public but Ryan was also becoming increasingly impatient with the military censor and Von Braun's fear of revealing too much. As Von Braun's spaceflight concepts were very much an unofficial interest, and he wasn't yet a US citizen, he feared being sent back to Germany in disgrace for having revealed classified missile technology.

Promotional poster for the Collier's series

This led to much frustration on the part of Ryan, who was busy preparing the material for an expanded book version to be called *Across the Space Frontier*. In a letter to Ryan dated 14th July 1952 the stressed Von Braun apologised for seeming to be a "miserable, uncooperative, double-crossing stinker" because of his own "constipated" desire to get fresh military clearance for their book – even though the material had already been published in the magazine.

By way of explanation he revealed that the CIA had recently interviewed him concerning the publication of his *Mars Project* book in Germany – the same book that had previously been rejected by seventeen American publishers before he gave up and sent it for publication in his homeland. Although Von Braun had been able to prove that this wasn't an obscure attempt to leak classified information, he was clearly rattled and let Ryan know about his concerns for the new book: "This situation really puts me on the spot," he wrote. "If this book comes out in September...I can be rightfully accused of disobeying a military directive...I can't take that risk. Not only would I expose myself to disciplinary action, the Department of Defense would probably throw a monkey-wrench into any further publications from my side. Connie, you are a hot reporter and a go-getter. I am in the Army. Despite the differences we did pretty well, to our mutual benefit, didn't we? So cool off, just a little bit, and realise that I have my problems too! In the end, everything will come out alright."

Luckily the military censor passed the book for publication and it was published as planned. Looking ahead, Von Braun observed to Ryan that there wouldn't be trouble with the next *Collier's* article about a manned moon landing (18th and 25th October 1952) as "in this piece the possibility of an objection or a cut can be ruled out as the army obviously has no business on the moon." With the publication of each new article, public interest increased and the magazine was flooded with letters asking about the men who would fly, so the team next looked at the training of these "spacemen" in its 28th March 1953 issue. Other reader-inspired features included articles about spacesuits (28th February 1953), and how a space crew might be saved in an emergency (14th March 1953).

As the popularity of the space series grew, there appears to have been friction between Ryan and Von Braun's traditional collaborators – Willy Ley and Chesley Bonestell.

In his own encyclopaedic history of the period, Willy Ley plays down Ryan's involvement, to the point of failing to mention him by name. He refers to the reporter in an underhand way by commenting that "articles on unmanned satellites slowly grew...among them was one in *Collier's* (27th June 1953); unfortunately the staff writer who 'edited' it suppressed nearly all the technical information."

Chesley Bonestell wrote to Von Braun many years later that he was "sorry to see that our friend Connie Ryan has made a tremendous success of his books...where he was impossible before, he must by now be intolerable!"

Ron Miller, Bonestell's biographer, believes this was just a sign of his relationship with all editors: "I don't think that Bonestell's relationship with Ryan was any frostier that it was with anyone else. Bonestell liked very much playing the role of the crusty curmudgeon and his recollections of most people are filtered through that persona...even people he was very close to. It is true, too, that Bonestell had little patience with anyone he thought less knowledgeable about certain subjects than he thought they ought to be. He also had a great disregard for anyone who was in a superior position to him, particularly if he fell into that previously mentioned category."

At the beginning of their collaboration together Von Braun might have only seen Ryan as a means to an end but the two do seem to have become friends. The first of their articles were being written shortly after the birth of the reporter's first child, so when told that his young son was having difficulty sleeping Von Braun advised that a half-a-teaspoon of whiskey into the child's bottle would help. Although Ryan had been told the same by his mother back in Dublin, it was only after the father of the American rocket programme repeated it that he dared do it.

Ryan also helped Von Braun out by arranging for him to be paid $1,500 per article – a great help for a scientist on a modest civil servant's salary. Their friendship also paid off when criticism of Von Braun's space plans turned personal. When *Time* magazine's science correspondent Jonathan Leonard attacked Von Braun in his book *Flight into Space*, Ryan defended him, writing: "Glibly and slickly he snipes and belittles Von Braun...there is still a great need for a really critical and constructive appraisal of Von Braun's theories (but) Mr. Leonard's book does not fill that bill. Indeed, for a book on space travel it never really gets off the ground." [75]

But Ryan's enthusiasm for spaceflight eventually waned – perhaps as a result of one too many comments by his *Collier's* colleagues that he was becoming the "poet laureate of the space cadet brigade". [76]

These tensions finally came into the open in the summer of 1953 when a final article on a manned mission to Mars was scheduled. When Willy Ley and Bonestell revealed that they had signed their own book contract for a Mars book, Ryan was furious at their apparent attempt to block him from the book deal. Neither side would back down and the feature, originally due for publication in late 1953, was delayed by six months and was released without the usual publicity, a sure sign that *Collier's* had finally lost interest.

Although still a cover story in the 30th April 1954 issue, the Mars article turned out to be the most downbeat of the series – admitting that a manned mission to Mars was still a "century away". With this honest prediction the enormously influential *Collier's* spaceflight series, which had captured the public's imagination with a series of eight spectacular features, came to an end.

The Longest Day 1959

By the mid-1950s the editorial department of *Collier's* was under the benevolent control of Roger Darkin, a shy editor who shunned foreign affairs and preferred wordy articles. Indeed, by 1954 the motto at the magazine was "scope not scoop". [77]

Darkin assembled a group of Bostonians around himself, and Ryan was regarded as one of this "older brother group" by the young writers. Darkin also encouraged his team to explore more human-interest angles to their stories. His belief that good writing would find its own audience was a dream to the writers. Whilst still concentrating on military themed articles (often about cutting-edge technology) Ryan tried his hand at the new narrative reporting style first pioneered by Walter Lord in his classic *Titanic* book *A Night To Remember*, which was first serialised in *Collier's*. Ryan's later articles explored the death of an Indy Car race driver, the ditching of a Pan Am plane in the Pacific Ocean, and the sinking of the *Andrea Doria* passenger liner just off New York. In retrospect these were prototypes for his later war books.

When visiting the Normandy beaches in 1949 as a part of an all-expenses-paid junket for ex-war correspondents dubbed 'D-Day Revisited', Ryan first had the idea for a book on the first 24 hours of the Allied invasion of Hitler's Europe. He combined this passion to tell the stories of the first soldiers to arrive on the beaches of France with a determination to produce a volume that was so accurate that it would not be torn to shreds by professional historians.

Although *The Longest Day* would finally appear in 1959 as 90,000 finely crafted words and become an instant hit, if Ryan had realized the despair that he would often go through in trying to complete the book he might have dropped the idea on the beaches of Normandy in June 1949.

Ryan's first attempt to tackle the story of D-Day in a longer format was an article he wrote for *Collier's* magazine in 1956 entitled 'The Major of St. Lo'. It revolved around events as US troops liberated the small French town of St. Lo. Shortly after the major in question had given the order to advance, he was killed but his troops still carried his body so that he could be amongst his men. Ryan had witnessed the distraught soldiers place the flag-draped body on the altar of the cathedral and the incident had caught his imagination. Years later he set out to interview the soldiers involved, but his determination to move the story beyond reportage meant he rewrote the article nine times before he felt ready to publish it.

"I knew one day I would write the story about him," he admitted. "It took me almost twelve years to do it. Factually it is right, but I am still not entirely satisfied with it. You always think when writing about a man like [Major] Howie that you ought to do more." [78]

'The Major of St. Lo' was an icebreaker for Ryan's D-Day book idea, and was optioned by a television station and dramatized as a 30 minute play starring actor Peter Graves in 1955.

As noted above, an important influence on Ryan was Walter Lord's retelling of the sinking of the *Titanic* in *A Night to Remember*. This book not only directly influenced Ryan's approach to telling a historic event in virtual real-time but also created the market for such "narrative history". [79] Lord's technique of covering a well-known topic through the eyes of many of those taking part set the template and Ryan realised that he could bring his own journalism skills to the retelling of the first 24 hours of D-Day.

The editors at *Collier's* also saw the commercial potential of Lord's "narrative faction" style. The biggest of these stories literally sailed into New York in late July 1956 when the Italian cruise-liner *Andrea Doria* struck a Norwegian vessel as it approached the city and sank. It was like the sinking of the *Titanic* in slow motion, with the cameras there to watch. The magazine couldn't compete with the immediacy of television but a small paragraph in the *New York Times* caught the eye of a senior editor and Ryan was tasked with telling the tragic story of the death of a Dr. Peterson's wife in Cabin 56. It would be a cover story and he only had two weeks to do it. Furthermore, he had to do it in Lord's style. To do this Ryan and his team began to ring as many of the survivors as they could for their own perspectives on the event.

"It was a slow business, but gradually we began to build a research file," explained Ryan. "Night and day the job went on until a chronology began to emerge which gave us a minute-by-minute account of what had happened."

Ryan even visited the *Andrea Doria*'s sister ship the *Christoforo Columbo* to measure out the various scenes of the story and understand the movements of the people involved.

After a frantic week's work, they had amassed a file of over 150,000 words. Ryan booked a room in the Waldorf Astoria and locked himself away. His skills as a 'hack' enabled him to churn out the story in five days. It was on the newsstands as the cover feature of the 28th September issue, less than six weeks after the accident. The article proved a sensation with the public and sold an extra 900,000 copies. It was later dramatised as a one-hour play by NBC television's Armstrong Circle Theater. [80]

As fellow writer Theodore H. White would say of the change in style for Ryan: "He had been persuaded to try his hand at a different style of narrative, the episode-by-episode recreation of large events. This style served *Collier's* well in its closing months as Ryan perfected it and brought to his reporting a quality that later produced his memorable books."

Even though Ryan was one of the stars of the magazine, as he recalled later, when he told his colleagues of his idea for a D-Day book they pointedly asked him if he was "mad". [81]

Although Ryan's star was now at its zenith, he and the other writers at *Collier's* were totally ignorant of the magazine's bleak future. By 1956 the simple fact was that television was attracting more advertising money. In 1951 *Collier's* had sold a total of 1,718 pages of advertising during the year, but by 1955 that total had dropped to 1,008 pages. At $22,000 per advertising page, it was a huge amount of money. As a result, the annual accounts were tens of millions of dollars less than they had been at the start of the decade.

When news of the financial crisis finally filtered down to the editorial department, the writers did what they thought would attract more readers, but unfortunately this only speeded the magazine's demise. Ironically, in doing their best to boost circulation, the writers were effectively cutting their own throats. The simple fact was that more readers actually cost the publishers more money, as each issue sold on the newsstand was sold at a loss. Each magazine cost *Collier's* 25 cents to print and another 20 cent to distribute, but had a cover price of 15 cents.

Although the rest was meant to be made up by advertising, this was declining as companies switched over to television. Bizarrely, each copy of the magazine that was sold cost the publisher around 25 cents, and the newly increased circulation added a $100,000 per issue loss each month!

The inevitable boardroom decision to close *Collier's* was made on Tuesday 11th December 1956, taking the editorial office completely by surprise. When staff were informed late on Friday evening, many broke down in tears. The situation wasn't made any easier by the presence of television cameras roaming the office trying to interview the staff about the situation. Ironically, the *Collier's* on the newsstands at that time had a cover story by Ryan entitled 'One Minute to Ditch'.

Ryan now found himself jobless, just when he was trying to make sense of a mountain of privately funded D-Day research for his planned book. It is hardly surprising that he was briefly hospitalised for a recurrence of the malaria that he had contracted during his time in Japan. Although the Du Pont Corporation offered him a well-paid public relations job, he bravely decided to work on his D-Day project full-time, with his wife offering to support them financially with her *House and Home* job until the book was published. [82]

When Ryan approached the US Army looking for a list of soldiers who had taken part in D-Day he was told that no such list existed. If he wanted to interview men who had taken part in the invasion he would have to find them himself. He started by placing an ad in various veterans' magazines with a list of questions and a request for people to contact him.

The questionnaire included questions such as:

What is your full name?
What were your unit and division?
Where did you arrive in Normandy, and at what time?
What was your rank on 6th June 1944?
What was your age on 6th June 1944?
Were you married at that time?
What is your wife's name?
Did you have any children at that time?
What do you do now?
When did you know that you were going to be part of the invasion?
What was the trip like during the crossing of the Channel? Do you remember, for example, any conversations you had or how you passed the time?
What were the rumours on board the boat, ship or plane in which you made the crossing?
Did you by any chance keep a diary of what happened to you on that day?
Were any of your friends killed or wounded either during the landing or during the day?
Do you remember any conversations you had with them before they became casualties?
Were you wounded?
Do you remember what it was like; that is, do you remember whether you felt any pain or were you so surprised that you felt nothing?
Do you recall any incident, sad or heroic, or simply memorable, which struck you more than anything else?
In times of great crisis, people generally show either great ingenuity or self-reliance; others do incredibly stupid things. Do you remember any examples of either?
Where were you at midnight on 5th June 1944?
Where were you at midnight on 6th June 1944?
Do you know of anybody else who landed within those 24 hours (midnight 5th June to midnight 6th June) as infantry, glider or airborne troops, or who took part in the air and sea operations?

To Ryan's immense surprise he received hundreds of replies, but this flood of information combined with his own perfectionism soon made the writer despair if he would ever get to the bottom of the story.

"Many, many times he gave up and threw it in the corner and said it could never be done because there was too much research involved," his brother Gerard recalled. "I suppose at that time Kathryn was the most help to him." [83]

On the verge of giving up, Ryan approached the *Reader's Digest* publishing empire with the suggestion that it use its vast network of international bureaus to help interview veterans who had responded to his earlier questionnaire. The author knew that to do so himself would add countless years to his research. DeWitt Wallace, the *Reader's Digest* owner not only accepted Ryan's request but also agreed to fund the overall research bill in return for first publication rights to the book when it was eventually written.

Tragically, as Ryan was finishing the writing of his D-Day book, his sister Kathleen, a Pan Am air stewardess, was drowned off the African coast during a stopover for the airline. As the only daughter in the family, her death was especially hard on the Ryan family, and Cornelius flew to Africa to personally return her body to Dublin.

Like her mother, Kathleen had trained as a teacher but many of her brothers felt she was too sensitive for the profession and was often deeply affected by the desperate situations she encountered daily in the schools around inner-city Dublin. She often came home crying because another promising student had been pulled out of class when they were old enough to work. In an effort to persuade them otherwise, Kathleen often visited the parents to plead that they let the child continue their education at school.

When she finally quit and took up the air stewardess position at Pan Am, everyone was relieved. She was soon thriving, travelling the world and even got engaged to a doctor in New York, but then tragedy struck in 1958 on that stopover in the Ivory Coast (now Ghana). Unfortunately she was the first into the notoriously current-plagued seas when her flight crew decided to go to the beach and was swept out to sea.

Kathleen Ryan

"I was the unfortunate one who picked up the phone," lamented her brother David. "I was so shocked that I wasn't sure what had happened. I thought they said she'd been kidnapped but eventually the terrible realisation came that they had been telling me that she had been drowned." When the news reached Cornelius, he rang contacts in Washington, pleading for them to put pressure on the Africans to find her still missing body. By the time it washed up on a local beach several days later, Ryan was already in Accra. To his dismay, he literally had to fight officials to get her body flown out of the country as quickly as possible. [84]

Upon arrival, the plane made three circles of their home city in her honour. It must have been a heart-breaking moment for Ryan to return to Dublin with the body of his only sister. As a mark of respect, air hostesses from all the other airlines lined the route out of the airport along with young children from the schools in which she had taught. Although Kathleen's loss was a terrible blow, her mother still displayed her own strong character during the funeral ceremony when the mother of another Irish air hostess killed in a plane crash several years earlier approached in a distressed state.

"My mother ended up comforting this woman on the morning of her own daughter's funeral," recalled Gerard Ryan.

After Kathleen was buried in the family plot at Mount Jerome Cemetery in Harold's Cross, Cornelius flew to New York for the official Pan Am memorial, but left immediately afterwards to avoid any further commiserations from well-wishers. His wife found him many hours later in their apartment, hard at work on the final draft pages of *The Longest Day*. [85]

The Longest Day was immensely popular when it was published – just as Ryan had believed. It was also extremely successful in France because it focused on French resistance to the German occupation. The book sold 270,000 hardback copies there and even resulted in a 'fan letter' to Ryan from General Charles de Gaulle. [86]

Because of the book's success, Ryan himself soon became intertwined with the story and was inundated with letters from people who wanted to talk about the event. Sometimes these approaches were deeply disturbing for Ryan – especially when ex-soldiers would present themselves at his New York apartment and expect him to hear their confessionals. One deeply traumatized veteran admitted to Ryan that he had nearly made it through the entire war without firing a shot, only to accidently kill nine of his colleagues in a friendly fire incident. Another soldier admitted that he enjoyed sneaking up behind German soldiers to slit their throats. [87]

Cold War 1960-69

John F. Kennedy's campaign team for the 1960 presidential election had a tight-knit, intimate feel to it because many were Irish-Americans eager to prove that they were just as good as the WASP bluebloods. This underdog mentality, combined with the existing Kennedy 'can do' spirit, helped this Irish Catholic clique get into the White House for the first time. Kennedy's pressman Pierre Salinger – a colleague of Ryan's on *Collier's* – called on his Dublin-born buddy to help him set up a press centre for the dozens of reporters who flocked to Hyannis Port on election day. The local National Guard armoury was commandeered, whilst a television dealer was persuaded to lend a dozen television sets and a Ford dealership provided ten new Thunderbirds for the staff. Bizarrely, the local Catholic church refused to provide benches to seat the reporters, so they had to ask a Protestant church instead.

During the night of the election, Bobby's house on the Kennedy compound was the official headquarters of the JFK vote-analysis team. [88] For this purpose, a vote-tabulating machine was set up in his main dining room, around which everyone assembled as the first votes started to come in. As results from the eastern states seemed very positive for Kennedy, Ryan must have imagined he would be driving the President Elect down to the press centre soon enough, but amid the constant ringing of phones the atmosphere grew sombre as it became evident the vote was tight. What had at first seemed like a victory was in danger of becoming a Kennedy defeat. By 3.30 am nobody knew if Kennedy was president or not. Like everyone else, they had to rely on the television pundits (likely Walter Cronkite) to give them the latest news from around the country. [89]

As JFK sat motionless in his chair watching television, he uttered the occasional curse when the results were bad. When he could take no more, he announced that he was off to bed and was escorted across the dark lawn of the compound to his quarters. Ironically, as he walked in-step with history Ryan's reporting skills deserted him momentarily and he misheard

Kennedy say he was "angry" when what he had said was that he was "hungry". [90]

JFK awoke at 7.30 am to be told that he had won the election and shortly thereafter was driven by Ryan to meet the assembled media as the new President.

Kennedy would later have his writer friend in mind on the day of his official inauguration, when he shared an awkward car ride with ex-President Dwight Eisenhower. In an effort to break the ice, Kennedy mentioned *The Longest Day* and was taken aback when the former general replied that he hadn't read the book because he'd been there on D-Day! [91]

Ryan looks on as Kennedy celebrates

Around this time legendary Hollywood producer Richard Darryl Zanuck gained the rights to *The Longest Day* in a peculiar way but on reading it became convinced of its movie potential. Although French producer Raoul Levy had initially optioned the book from the publishers for $25,000, he failed to get a movie deal off the ground and signed the rights over to Paris-based Zanuck to pay off a debt. Zanuck contacted the author to work on a script, but their working relationship can best be described as a clash of egos.

Zanuck needed Ryan's encyclopaedic knowledge of the invasion, whilst Ryan needed Zanuck's money. Zanuck was offering Ryan $100,000 for full-rights to make the book, and the author naturally accepted. They met face-to-face in New York in December 1960, but their attitudes to each other were described as "a peculiar mixture of admiration and antagonism that was to set the tone of their future relationship." [92] By January 1961 Ryan was in Paris working on the film script but Zanuck's style irritated the writer. In script conferences, Zanuck would pace around the room imagining dialogue and scenes – which would be transcribed into a script by secretaries. Ryan soon lost patience with this approach.

"We sat there like so many dummies, and then 'Darryl Eisenhower' would dictate to us what happened on D-Day," Ryan later told Zanuck biographer Mel Gussow, who accurately portrays the author's frustration that 'Cornelius Ryan's The Longest Day' was quickly becoming 'Darryl Zanuck's The Longest Day'.

When Ryan finished the script in mid-1961 he returned to the US, but he was soon furious to learn that Zanuck had brought in five other writers (Romain Gary, James Jones, Erich Remarque, David Pursall and Jack Seddon) to rework it. Worse, in the titles the story would be credited to 'Gary, Jones, Pursall, Seddon and Ryan'.

An insulted Ryan immediately went to the Writers' Guild, which ordered Zanuck to award the writer sole credit for the screenplay. The favourable portrayal of the French resistance in the movie resulted in the authorities agreeing to Zanuck's request for a lavish premier in the centre of Paris in September 1962 – with fifty French tanks rolling past the cinema

Talking with Irish UN troops at Dublin Airport, 1962

accompanied by divisions from each of the allied armies involved in the D-Day invasion. After the movie, the Eiffel Tower erupted in a massive fireworks display and Edith Piaf made a rare appearance to sing to the watching crowds. Considering all this effort, it is no surprise that Ryan held back on any lasting bitterness towards Zanuck. The movie went on to make $17 million during its first year and many credited it with saving the financially struggling 20th Century Fox studio. Right after the Paris premier, Ryan flew to Dublin for a special VIP screening for his friends and family at the Ambassador cinema. As he descended the steps of his plane at Dublin airport he must have finally felt some satisfaction to be returning home a conquering hero. "It was a big occasion," remembered David Ryan. "There was a feeling amongst Dubliners that 'their boy' had done an extraordinary thing and brought out a Hollywood film." [93]

After the huge success of *The Longest Day*, the pressure was on Ryan to come up with a worthy successor. Although he had wanted to write a book about the battle for Arnhem next, he quickly changed his plans when he was unexpectedly given permission by the Soviets to see their once secret war archives in Moscow. Although this would mean his planned World War Two set would be out of sequence, he grabbed this opportunity. His new aim was now to have a book about the Battle of Berlin ready to coincide with the 20th anniversary of the end of the war in May 1965. [94]

This change of direction would also bring him into conflict with fellow narrative historian John Toland, who had earlier agreed to drop a book on wartime OSS founder William Donovan after Ryan told him he was also planning a similar volume. Unfortunately, Toland dropped his Donovan book to work on a Berlin book – unaware that Ryan was now working on one too.

Using his high-profile contacts in the Kennedy administration Ryan had asked his friend General James Gavin, who had been recently appointed US Ambassador to Paris, to approach the Soviet authorities on his behalf. Although this had come to nothing, President Kennedy apparently opened the way for Ryan when he raised the issue directly with Soviet Premier Nikita Khrushchev during the Vienna summit.

In early 1963 Ryan received official permission to access the World War Two military archives in Moscow (possibility because the Soviets hoped he would give 'GI Ivan' the Hollywood treatment), their only pre-condition being that he couldn't take along another American researcher. The Soviets indicated that the University of Manchester academic John Erickson (an Englishman of Norwegian parents and married to a Yugoslav wife), was acceptable, so before they could change their minds Erickson was signed up by the *Reader's Digest* as Ryan's official translator and the two flew to Moscow in April 1963 on a three-week research trip.

"When Connie was in Russia he was insensitive because he didn't really know the Soviet Union," remembered Erickson's wife Ljubica. "John had to diplomatically extricate Ryan on a number of occasions because he was very forthright and combative. He didn't broker much opposition and if he wanted something he would ask and during those moments John had to calm things down." [95]

Another gaffe on Ryan's part was a question about General Vlasov, a Red Army commander who had formed an army of ex-Soviet prisoners in order to fight against the Red Army. When Ryan started to press the point his young research assistant quickly realised that even to mention this was a serious mistake and quickly changed the subject.

Ironically Ryan's tough approach might have been influenced by a pep-talk he received from President Kennedy just before his trip during which JFK told the author that the Russians were "horse traders" at heart. Ryan later acknowledged his methods were not as diplomatic as they might have been.

Sensing that Erickson could steer Ryan away from embarrassing topics, the Soviets produced several 'stars' of the Red Army for them to interview – including Commander of the First Ukrainian Front Marshal Ivan S. Koniev, Commander of the Second Belorussian Front Marshal Konstantin K. Rokossovskii, Tank Corp Commander Major General Ivan I. Yushchuk, and Rifle Division Battalion Commander General Konstantin Y. Samsonov, who had captured the Reichstag.

"Once we'd started, the difficulty was in getting them to stop talking," recalled Erickson later. "The interviews went on not merely for hours but for days."

One controversial subject that Ryan was determined to get an answer to was the mass rape of German women by Red Army troops. Before the trip both the US State Department and the British Foreign Office had advised him not to raise the topic, but Kennedy urged him to "lay it on the table".

Although the Soviets repeatedly refused to discuss this, an emotional outburst by Erickson made them change their mind.

When the Englishman reminded them that his Serbian wife had been liberated by Soviet troops and that the last thing he wanted to do was tarnish the reputation of the average Red Army soldier they finally admitted it had happened. [96]

This huge scoop was quickly followed by an even bigger one when Marshal Vasili D. Sokolovskii rather matter-of-factly mentioned that the Red Army had found Hitler's body in Berlin in May 1945 – despite years of official denials by Moscow.

When their research trip was finally over, they were given tickets to watch the official May Day military parade in Red Square prior to their departure. Despite their VIP status, airport officials tried unsuccessfully to confiscate their hard-won interview notes and documents, and it wasn't until their plane touched down in Paris that they felt safe. Even then, a homesick Erickson wanted to fly directly back to England to see his wife and only agreed to remain in Paris when the *Reader's Digest* agreed to fly her over to Paris to help finish translating the Russian documentation. They were all put up in a top Parisian hotel, with Ryan so amazed at the double room given to the Ericksons that he contacted the magazine asking for an upgrade too.

A press conference was quickly organised to announce what they had discovered in Moscow and the story made headlines worldwide – except in Eastern Europe where writer John Toland was making his own way to see the Moscow archives. Unfortunately, Ryan's mention of the rape of German women put Toland in an awkward position and when he eventually arrived at the Russian embassy in Budapest to pick up his prearranged visa for Moscow he was stunned to be told he was no longer welcome in the Soviet Union. Only later did he discover this was official Kremlin "retribution" for Ryan's indiscretions. [97]

"When Ryan went to the Soviet Union he went with a preconceived idea, that was very clear, and he was going to support that idea," believed Ljubica Erickson. "What he needed was not to learn about what they were like, what he needed was the factual details about the battle from the east to the west. I think he already knew how he was going to describe it before he went."

Despite their difference of opinions on Russia, the Ericksons and Ryan enjoyed a good personal relationship. John Erickson even went so far as to acknowledge that the trip had given him contacts in the Soviet military that resulted in his two classic histories *The Road to Stalingrad* (1975) and *The Road to Berlin* (1982).

"I liked Connie and got on well with him, but he was demanding," said Ljubica Erickson. "He was good company, with lots of jokes but he didn't seem like a relaxed man. He was full of nervous energy. Although he was proud to have come from Ireland he was more American than an American."

Ryan next flew to Dublin, staying at the famed Shelbourne Hotel on St. Stephen's Green – where Hitler's half-brother Alois had once worked as a waiter! Aware that President Kennedy was due in the Irish capital shortly he sought out a meeting with Taoiseach (Prime Minister) Sean Lemass. As a friend of President Kennedy, the meeting was officially to brief the Irish Prime Minister about his visit behind the Iron Curtain, but it had as much to do with the US President's imminent visit and Ryan's lobbying to become the American Ambassador to Ireland during JFK's second term.

"Kennedy thought a great deal of Con and I'm sure he would've made him Ambassador," was Gerard Ryan's opinion of what at first seems an improbable idea. "Of course, he was also playing the 'two ends against the middle', as Con was an Irish success story as well as an American one." [98]

His brother David remembered Cornelius being very much a Kennedy man, even though he was wise to Kennedy's personal problems: "Con was very much a Democrat but knew Kennedy for what he was – a womaniser like his father. He did have great admiration for the President, but like anyone in an inner circle he knew about the other side of Kennedy."

In mid-July Ryan visited the White House with all the inside details of his dealings with the Kremlin horse-traders. The conversation must have been a fascinating one, with the President on a high after his own deeply felt 'homecoming' trip to Ireland. JFK showed the author a green leather-bound book presented to him by Taoiseach Lemass which contained a copy of the land deeds for the Kennedy clan in Wexford. "Isn't that beautiful," the young President enthused. [99]

Ryan left the White House promising his friend a copy of an interview tape he had done with Eisenhower, but the two would never meet again.

"He telephoned within minutes of the assassination and was in tears on the other end of the line," remembered David Ryan. "He was shattered and very upset." JFK's death put an end to any dream (however realistic) of an ambassadorial posting after the publication of *The Last Battle*.

With his Soviet scoop safe, Ryan turned to the central German core of the story when he went in search of Hitler's ex-generals. As they had on *The Longest Day* his *Reader's Digest* team contacted ordinary Germans, both civilians and soldiers, who were caught up in the final days of that battle, and Ryan gained access to senior ex-generals using his contacts in the US and West German militaries. Ryan found his central character for the book in the form of Colonel General Gotthard Heinrici, known as the 'Defender of Berlin'.

Ultimately, the book missed its 1965 deadline and actually appeared after Toland's *The Last 100 Days*, but by the time Ryan attended the Frankfurt International Book Fair in October 1966 his book had been on the US bestsellers list for seven weeks and was still selling 5,000 hardback copies a week. The total European sales were in excess of 500,000 copies. [100]

Ryan's affection for German General Heinrici caused much criticism, with official US Army historian S. L. A. ('Slam') Marshall saying in the *New York Times Book Review* that he preferred Toland's account of the battle. Marshall was most sceptical of Ryan's judgment when it came to what the Germans were telling him. "If the story of the German defeat on the Oder was to be told, the recall of a number of superannuated German commanders had to be trusted. One must simply take it with salt – if there is enough of that commodity around," Marshall opined. "It is a beguiling portrait, questionable only because Heinrici and entourage are the main sources. Old warriors attract Ryan almost immoderately, and he paints them well."

Many reviewers also thought the book was too influenced by Cold War rhetoric. Readers got the sense that the author was secretly rooting for the Berliners, whom he portrayed as having been abandoned in the first mistake of the Cold War. Not surprisingly, the most vicious review was published in the official Red Army newspaper *Krasnaya Zvezda*.

The writer at the height of his success

In an article entitled 'Ryan's Last Battle – Slander or Delusion?' its writer suggested: "Throughout the entire book, Ryan engages in mud-slinging, having as his target the Soviet Army, its officers and men. He seeks out and stresses isolated failures of the Soviet troops, describing with relish any mistake he comes across, searching everywhere for intrigues. He does this, as a rule by quoting Nazi generals, using them as mouthpieces for his own ideas. Ryan is piddling in the backyard of history, trying to find another piece of mud to sling at the Soviet people and their army." When the Soviets revealed their own official take on the discovery of Hitler's body in a 1969 book, they again used it to take a shot at Ryan.

"Every Soviet officer and soldier who fought during those exciting days with the 1st Byelorussian or the 1st Ukrainian Front knows the importance of the battle for Berlin. Only Mr. Cornelius Ryan, author of the American bestseller *The Last Battle*, seems unaware of it. His version is the preferred one of all those who wish to prove that the strategic capacity of Soviet generals isn't really so great, compared with the achievements of the defenders of Berlin or the strategic capacities of American generals who would have found it easy to conquer that last citadel of the dying German Reich." [101]

Although the film rights had been snapped up by MGM in 1964, by the end of the decade the Americans had grown tired of war movies because they could see a real life one on their televisions each night. The cinema-going public was trying to escape the mess of Vietnam, and Hollywood quickly realised that a big gung-ho World War Two epic wasn't likely to go down well with a more cynical public. The late 1960s seemed as far from 1962 as the battle for Berlin itself.

In one last desperate attempt to get the book made into a movie, Bob O'Brien, the new head of MGM, commissioned a script from Ryan in late 1968. To save money, the studio planned to produce two Berlin movies – Ryan's *Last Battle* and Leon Uris' war novel *Armageddon* – with Ryan working on both scripts at once. Even though Ryan hated Uris' novel, he had to agree to the deal because it was the only chance for his own book to be filmed. Ryan even relocated to California for a short period to be near the movie producers, but in late

1969 he was finally told MGM was calling time on their option for his Battle of Berlin book.

But history also has a strange sense of timing, one which saw him fly down to Cape Kennedy in July 1969 to watch the launch of Apollo 11. Ryan had not only made the German rocket scientist Von Braun a household name in the 1950s but had also been involved in the campaign to elected President Kennedy - the man who finally enabled Von Braun to go to the Moon. Now that friendship allowed him to call in a favour and he covered the historic mission for *Reader's Digest*.

"For six incredible days during the lunar shot, I was Von Braun's right arm, bag carrier, and above all friend. During that time I doubt either of us slept more than three hours a night. And I was proud, on this momentous occasion, to have sat by his side, to have carried his bag." [102]

Battling Cancer 1970-74

After his unexpected detour on *The Last Battle*, Ryan's interest returned to his idea of a book about 1944's ill-fated Operation Market Garden to seize the bridge across the Rhine at Arnhem, and in 1967 he signed a contract to write 'The Big Drop', its original working title. [103]

Unlike *The Longest Day*, which was researched and written a decade or so after the battle, he would now be tackling a subject that was nearly 25 years old. Thankfully, he once again had the backing of the vast *Reader's Digest* network, and its foreign bureau staff managed to find 1,200 eyewitnesses through veterans' groups and ads in local newspapers, of whom 600 were interviewed. The *Digest* also financed several research trips to Europe by Ryan to visit battle locations and interview veterans.

At the higher end of the interview scale, the author interviewed his friend General James Gavin, former Allied Commander Ike Eisenhower, Field-Marshal Bernard Montgomery, Dutch underground leader Prince Bernhard and a host of their former German enemies. Bizarrely, when he tracked down former exiled Polish General Stanislaw Sosabowski he found him working as a labourer in England. [104]

Ryan's account reflected the American view that Operation Market Garden was doomed because of Montgomery, who was in operational command. In his interview Eisenhower called him a "psychopath", and Dutch Prince Bernhard pointedly remarked that his country could little afford another "Montgomery success" like Arnhem again.

"Cornelius thought he was a total egotist," remembered David Ryan. "Monty was told the tanks were too wide for the roadways, that the radio communications hadn't been tested and that nobody knew if they would work. You can set out a wonderful plan, but you have to listen to people who tell you the weaknesses." And "The object of the book wasn't to ruin Monty's reputation; he just set out the facts of the event.

If *A Bridge Too Far* showed Monty's weakness as a general then so be it. There wasn't any malice there." [105]

Fellow World War Two reporter Walter Cronkite related to Ryan the humorous tale of being followed by a group of US soldiers into Holland after he crash-landed in an American glider. Cronkite quickly discovered that he had mistakenly picked up a lieutenant's helmet in the confusion!

Although *A Bridge Too Far* was Cronkite's favourite World War Two book – partly because he was so proud of his own Dutch heritage – he always joked that he was a little sore at Ryan for using one of his best war anecdotes. "I was kind of sorry that he told it as I was hoping to tell it in my book, as I hadn't written it yet." [106]

Work on the Arnhem book stalled in 1969. Although the research files were ready, Ryan kept putting off starting to write it. Although his wife thought he was just depressed because of MGM's decision to back out of the movie version of *The Last Battle*, Ryan himself felt tired and believed old age was finally catching up with him. [107]

The first signs that his lethargy was a symptom of something more serious came during a holiday to see friends in the Caribbean in early 1970. When he arrived back in Connecticut his family doctor, a fellow Dubliner named Pat Neligan, spotted a hardening of his prostate gland and referred him for more tests.

Around this time Ryan finally started work on the Arnhem book, chiding himself for not having started it earlier. Shortly afterwards Ryan learned he had cancer. Nevertheless, he decided the best course of action was to concentrate on the book while undergoing treatment.

By the time of his 50th birthday on 5th June 1970, the gravity of his situation became clear when a specialist in New York recommended a radical prostatectomy that would probably leave him impotent and/or incontinent.

Ryan reasoned that his reluctance to start writing the new book was subconsciously related to his body's internal battle with cancer. There also appears to have been a lingering worry in his mind that his cancer might have been caused by radiation exposure during the two atomic bomb tests that he witnessed a quarter of a century earlier.

"He never said he believed he might have got the cancer from radiation exposure at the Bikini Atoll tests, but I did hear him talk about people who were dying from cancers picked up during the experiments in Nevada. I think mentally he had made the connection himself," his brother David pointed out. "There was no known family knowledge of cancer. My father died at a young age of 52 but not from cancer. Con was a big smoker but he looked after his health. He had medical check-ups twice a year and took vitamins religiously. He even had a full set of teeth when he died." [108]

Doctors soon had more bad news, as the cancer was spreading quickly. Ryan was advised that if nothing was done immediately he had only three years to live. In October 1970 several radioactive 'seeds' were inserted in the affected area to try and kill the cancer cells and he was handed a bill for $3,000 when he was discharged from hospital several days later.

In an effort to cheer him up, writer friend Harold Robbins stayed at the family home and kept Ryan busy with two script ideas. One was a bizarre TV show centred on the adventures of a James Bond-style roving reporter, whilst the other told the story of the 1966 blowing up of Nelson's Pillar in his native Dublin. [109]

By mid-1971 Ryan had only completed 47 pages of the Arnhem book, and in late summer the doctors told him X-rays had revealed that his right kidney had stopped functioning. This put too much of a strain on Kathryn, and she was hospitalised for ten days after having collapsed at home on 15th October suffering from exhaustion.

On a Caribbean cruise with his wife and daughter Victoria in March 1972, he told Kathryn that he didn't know whether it would be possible for him to finish the book. This was a major worry for the family, since if the book wasn't finished before he died the publishers' advance would have to be repaid. At that very moment, all they were surviving on were royalties from sales of *The Longest Day* and *The Last Battle*. [110]

In the spring of 1972 another bone scan revealed that the cancer had spread to Ryan's right hip, left thighbone, chest vertebrae and rib cage. He was now 'officially dying', but his desire to live a little longer in order to finish the book led him to try a course of treatment that he would normally have rejected – taking female hormones. At that time Ryan confided to his secret taped diary that he was shocked to discover that his wife had hidden all the ammunition for his guns. On Friday 27th April 1973 the latest set of tests hinted that the cancer had spread to his bone marrow.

As chemotherapy was still a new science in the early 1970s, patients were really guinea pigs for new treatments. Ryan's first session started on Monday 30th April, but by early June he was in so much pain in his lower body that he was confined to a wheelchair. Although he found the whole thing depressing he continued to work on the book each day. A suggestion by his wife that she would be able to finish the book if he couldn't simply spurred the highly competitive writer to work harder. Nevertheless, as a precaution he dictated a full outline of the book to his private secretary Anne Bardenhagen. [111]

Ryan was too sick to leave his bed on his 53rd birthday, and received a stream of well-wishers who came to cheer him up. News of his illness had now reached many of his closest friends and his mail was also filled with light-hearted gifts designed to raise his mood. Walter Cronkite sent Ryan one of his own prized possessions – a piece of marble mounted on a wall-plaque with the words 'Hitler Stood Here' written underneath.

"I got into Hitler's eastern headquarters in Poland after it had been bombed and picked up a wonderful fist-sized memento from his house. There were American guards all around, but I sneaked it into my bag," remembered Cronkite. "Several months later I finally asked him if he had got the birthday present. He said he 'guessed' he did. I was surprised and asked if he recognised it for what it was? He just said to me that it got to him broken and that he didn't want to say anything about it. He said it was just a broken piece of plaster.

It was then that I told him that it was a piece of the last urinal Hitler had in eastern Poland but he never did seem to get that joke!" [112] But at that moment, Ryan's dark mood was very much influenced by the fact that his own private medical bills were in the region of $70,000, something which would be a serious financial threat to his family if he couldn't complete the book in time.

By mid-June 1973 Ryan was back at his desk writing again when his mood was lightened somewhat by finding that, much to his surprise, the French President Georges Pompidou had awarded him the *Legion of Honour* – France's highest civilian decoration. On hearing of his terminal illness, friends and well-wishers in Paris had lobbied the authorities to award the writer the honour. Due to Ryan's fragile health, it was decided that the French Ambassador to America would visit his Connecticut home in early July to present the honour on behalf of President Pompidou. [113]

The letters that Ryan received from World War Two veterans offering congratulations on his award again lifted his mood, as he felt the honour was as much for them as for him.

On 21st August 1973 Ryan was also the subject of a testimonial by the Correspondents Fund of America. Although deeply touched by the event, he saw it as an unwelcome preview of his own wake. "I felt as if I was standing at my graveside listening to the good things people were saying about me. Right words. Wrong funeral. If they like the book, then I'll feel I deserved the tribute."

Unfortunately these relatively uplifting events during the late summer of 1973 were overshadowed by the news from Dublin on 30th September that his mother had died. He was too weak to make the journey to attend her funeral and instead threw all his energies into finishing the book, the final page of which an emotional Ryan handed over to his wife with a hug on Saturday 27th October 1973. In total *A Bridge Too Far* had taken 39 months to write, with a final research bill of $165,000 presented to the *Reader's Digest*.

Ryan busied himself making arrangements with publishers around the world, and even flew to Holland, France and

England with his wife and daughter in November to finalised contracts. Many of the people who had known him personally over the years were shocked by his appearance as none of them had known he had cancer.

In mid-June 1974 he was well enough to go to Holland for a reunion of the main characters he had written about in *A Bridge Too Far* to mark the 30th anniversary of Operation Market Garden that September.

The trip was in effect a larger version of the regular five-yearly D-Day correspondents' reunions that he had been taking part in since 1949. Those had recently come to an end after Pan Am stopped offering free flights to France but Ryan stepped in and asked his publisher to sponsor a similar event as a press junket for his new book. The publisher, with the help of KLM, organised tours of the main Arnhem battlefields in Holland, with many of Ryan's friends (General Gavin, Pierre Salinger, Bob Considine and Ben Wright etc.) added to a guest list that included General Ridgway, Prince Bernhard of the Netherlands and six Polish officers.

In reality the trip was another 'living wake' for the author, much to the disgust of some. They soon nicknamed the tour the "Ryan Express" and only grudgingly gave the author some slack as a dying man. Little did they know that he would be dead within six weeks. [114]

As soon as Ryan arrived home he was much in demand by the press, and although physically exhausted he did what he thought was his duty and publicised the book wherever he could. He appeared on the 'Today' television programme, attended a 'Book of the Month Club' event, gave several radio interviews and a speech at the Dutch Society in New York. On 16th October he fulfilled another obligation by attending a *Reader's Digest* luncheon, but was tactlessly introduced by the host as a cancer sufferer. Ryan showed his macabre sense of humour by retorting: "Gentlemen, I suffer from a terminal case…of greed!"

On 22nd October, when he arrived for a regular chemotherapy session at New York's Memorial Hospital, Ryan was too exhausted to leave and was given a private room on the fourth floor. Thankfully, doctors isolated any pain to his legs and he was relatively comfortable in bed. As his condition worsened he was buoyed up by a steady stream of celebrity visitors. It all came to an end at 6 pm on 23rd November. His last words were: "I'm so damned tired."

Although there was talk of a military grave in Arlington Cemetery, Ryan was instead buried in Ridgefield, Connecticut under a small gravestone that simply says 'Cornelius Ryan – 1920-1974 – Reporter'.

As he knew that he would never see it himself, shortly before he died the author had ensured that *A Bridge Too Far* would make it to the movie screen by signing over the rights to maverick Hollywood producer Joseph Levine. Perhaps bitter at the failure to get *The Last Battle* made into a film, the author accepted Levine's large up-front payment on the condition that Levine would "do it justice". Their agreement would also see Ryan's widow acting as a technical consultant whilst his young son Geoffrey was employed as an assistant – a career he would later take up professionally.

For Levine, like Zanuck before him, Ryan's book would become an obsession and he personally bankrolled the production of the movie to the tune of $22 million. A dozen Hollywood stars and the hottest scriptwriter were signed up to add some showbiz, while an audience that was growing increasingly tired of real warfare would be placated by the use of veteran 'anti-war' director Richard Attenborough.

Screenwriter William Goldman would later say that whilst he was happy to have 650 pages of "fabulous material" to work with, he was placed under enormous pressure because the producer had already set a June 1977 release date even before he had finished the first draft of the script. Shooting began in Holland during the summer of 1976 with the Goldman script essentially portraying *A Bridge Too Far* as a classic "cavalry-to-the-rescue" story starring Gene Hackman, Robert Redford and Ryan O'Neill.

Ironically, Goldman would later express his frustration that his script was attacked by the critics because many of the scenes were considered unbelievable – even though they had been taken right from the pages of the book. [115]

After her work on the movie was completed, Kathryn

compiled her husband's posthumous memoir *A Private Battle* using his secret tape recordings. Although she didn't explicitly mention a connection between Ryan's cancer and his attendance at the Bikini Atoll bomb tests in the book, Kathryn revealed to an interviewer at the time of its publication that it did trouble her. She wondered aloud why he had a particularly virulent form of cancer for a man of his age, and mentioned that a reporter friend who had also been at the tests had recently died of Leukemia. [116]

Kathryn's own swansong came when she accompanied President Ronald Reagan during his trip to Normandy in June 1984 to commemorate the 40th anniversary of D-Day. She later retired to Florida and died there aged 68 in 1993.

Reporter or Historian?

Cornelius Ryan might have been what we could call a 'court historian' for the American military - obvious examples include the anti-Red Army bias of *The Last Battle* and the negative Montgomery tone of *A Bridge Too Far* - but it is worth remembering that he also reminded US audiences of the British, Canadian and French contribution to D-Day.

"When the book *The Ugly American* came out I think he saw in it many things which he agreed with," opined his brother Gerard Ryan. "It did not stop him from living there, as he saw a tremendous greatness in America, but he was very much an East Coast man."

Although Ryan tried to project an image of the East Coast intellectual, at heart he was still a Jesuit scholar type with a strict approach to the craft of writing. Whilst *The Longest Day* had its own unique gestation in his New York apartment, the two later books came to life in his spacious house in Connecticut where Ryan and his wife worked together during a nine-to-five routine in a special 'writing shed' at the bottom of their garden. Sometimes even this heavy workload wasn't enough for the author and he returned late at night to work on a book.

"At the back of all that he was a man who, even though he was talented, had a very low self-esteem," believed his brother Gerard. "There is nothing to stop you having low self-esteem and a superiority complex at the same time – they nearly go hand-in-hand. That would be my summing up of my brother Con, a talented genius – you don't write three bestsellers in America without being a genius! – but by the same token he was a bit of a people pleaser."

Ryan certainly suffered snobbery from other historians, who viewed him as little more than a journalist who turned his attention to writing war books. It is indeed ironic that Ryan's extensive research files for his three war books, now housed at Ohio University, are used by professional historians because they now offer unique first-hand accounts from soldiers who took part in many famous World War Two battles.

Although Ryan became something of a household name in Ireland after the publication of *The Longest Day*, his reputation there has often been hindered by his own later successful self-invention as an 'American'. An example of this came in 1988 when an attempt by the Irish Tourist Board to erect a commemorative plaque outside his family home was blocked by the new owners because they feared it might attract too many American tourists!

In the end, perhaps it is better to be simply remembered as a "reporters' reporter" – especially by those who appreciated the amount of work that went into his three war books. The fact that two of their titles – 'a bridge too far' and 'the longest day' – have now entered the English language as everyday expressions might also have made him smile.

-oOo-

References:

[1] David Ryan interview, 1st November 2004.
[2] 'Our Peace Loving Irishman', *Collier's*, pg. 66, 17th March 1951.
[3] Gerard Ryan interview, 9th September 2004.
[4] John Ryan (cousin) interview, 11th November 2004.
[5] Elizabeth Ludlow interview, 28th January 2005.
[6] David Ryan interview, 1st November 2004.
[7] 'James Plunkett, RTÉ and Strumpet City', Ed Mulhall, www.rte.ie.
[8] Tommy Darragh interview, 17th November 2004.
[9] John Ryan (cousin) interview 11th November 2004.
[10] Gerard Ryan, 9th September 2004.
[11] David Ryan interview, 24th August 2004.
[12] *A Private Battle*, pg. 28
[13] Walter Cronkite interview, 2nd December 2004.
[14] *Censorship in Ireland*, Donal O'Drisceoil, pg. 209.
[15] File '2/136', Irish Military Archives.
[16] 'Eire's Troubles Not to be Cured By a General Election', *Daily Telegraph* 12th May 1944.
[17] Gerard Ryan interview, 9th September 2004.
[18] 'Watched Navy Pound French Coast', *Daily Telegraph* 7th June 1944.
[19] 'Pin-Point Bombing After Beachhead Request', *Daily Telegraph* 12th June 1944.
[20] 'In Flak-Swept Plane to Bomb Rennes', *Daily Telegraph* 13th June 1944.
[21] 'Saturation Bombing of German Tank Base', *Daily Telegraph* 16th June 1944.
[22] 'Cherbourg Burns After Great Air Onslaught', *Daily Telegraph* 23rd June 1944.
[23] 'Important Enemy Link with Paris Bombed', *Daily Telegraph* 26th June 1944.
[24] *A Private Battle*, pg. 28.
[25] 'London Day by Day', *Daily Telegraph* 18th April 1945.
[26] *Never a shot in Anger*, Barney Oldfield, pg. 162.
[27] Gerard Ryan interview, 9th September 2004.

[28] 'Red Tape Road to Berlin', *The Saturday Review*, 26th March 1966.
[29] *A Private Battle*, pg. 29.
[30] David Ryan interview, 24th August 2004.
[31] 'Trapped Nazi Armoured Column Wiped Out', *Daily Telegraph* 2nd August 1944.
[32] 'Three War Correspondents Freed Famous Town', *Daily Telegraph* 5th August 1944.
[33] 'Roads to Paris Black with Allied Columns', *Daily Telegraph* 19th August 1944.
[34] Walter Cronkite interview, 2nd December 2004.
[35] *Warcos*, Richard Collier, pg. 173.
[36] *No Woman's World*, Iris Carpenter, pg. 112.
[37] 'Speed of Allied Thrust Crushed Aisne Deference', *Daily Telegraph* 2nd August 1944.
[38] *A Bridge Too Far*, pg. 54.
[39] 'London Day by Day', *Daily Telegraph* 18th April 1945.
[40] 'Maginot Forts Fell With Hardly A Shot Fired', *Daily Telegraph* 14th August 1944.
[41] *Never a Shot in Anger*, Barney Oldfield, pg. 140.
[42] 'Biggest Robot Assembly Plant Captured', *Daily Telegraph* 21st September 1944.
[43] 'Enemy Surrender Fort Near Thionville', *Daily Telegraph* 16th November 1944.
[44] *Patton*, Ladislas Farago, pg. 672.
[45] *Patton: A Genius for War*, Carlo D'Este, pg. 680.
[46] *Battle of Bulge*, John Toland, pg. 269.
[47] '3rd Army Nears Wiltz', *Daily Telegraph* 8th January 1945.
[48] 'Rhine Villagers Have Taste for War', *Daily Telegraph* 14th March 1945.
[49] 'Wholesale Murders in Nazi Prison Camp', *Daily Telegraph* 9th April 1945.
[50] *Patton: Genius for War,* pg. 735.
[51] David Ryan interview, 1st September 2004.
[52] Gerard Ryan interview, 9th September 2004.
[53] 'Drama in Tojo's Room', *Daily Telegraph* 12th September 1945.
[54] *Star Spangled Mikado*, pg. 49.
[55] *Star Spangled Mikado*, Pg. 194.

[56] *Star Spangled Mikado*, pg. 201.
[57] *Star Spangled Mikado*, pg. 203
[58] *It's All News to Me*, Bob Considine 1967.
[59] 'Atomic Bomb No.5 is Exploded Under Sea', *Daily Telegraph* 25th July 1946.
[60] 'Jews Jump into Sea from Immigrant Ship', *Daily Telegraph* 24th September 1946.
[61] David Ryan interview, 1st September 2004.
[62] 'Troops in Battle to Board Refugee Ship', *Daily Telegraph* 27th November 1946.
[63] Memo held in Fulton Oursler Jr. papers, Georgetown University.
[64] Unpublished 1957 autobiographical piece intended for *American Weekly*, Ryan Collection, University of Ohio.
[65] 'US Article on Ireland – Protest', *Irish Press*, 19th March 1951.
[66] John Ryan (cousin) interview, 11th November 2004.
[67] 'Preview of the War We Do Not Want', *Collier's* 27th October 1951.
[68] 'Collier's goes to War', *Newsweek*, 29th October 1951.
[69] 'Collier's Reports a War', *Time*, 29 October 1951.
[70] *Murrow: His life and Times*, A. M. Sperber, pg. 369.
[71] 'Postscript to Collier's World War III', *The Nation*, 8th December 1951.
[72] 'The Write Stuff', Dominic Phelan, *Spaceflight* September 2007.
[73] *Blueprint for Space*, Fred Ordway (ed.), pg. 129.
[74] 'The Evolution of the Apollo Spacecraft', Dave Dooling, *Spaceflight* March 1974.
[75] 'Wilderness of the Stars', *The Saturday Review*, 16th January 1954.
[76] *In Search of History*, Theodore. H. White, pg. 402.
[77] 'What Killed Colliers?', Hollis Alpert, *Saturday Review* 11th May 1957.
[78] *One Minute to Ditch*, pg. 152.
[79] *The File*, Penn Kimball, pg. 297.
[80] *One Minute to Ditch*, pg. 159.
[81] 'Irishman starts this Paris night of spectacle', *Sunday Independent*, 30th September 1962.
[82] David Ryan interview, 1st November 2004.

[83] Gerard Ryan interview, 9th September 2004.
[84] Kathryn Ryan letter in Dublin Writer's Museum archive.
[85] *A Private Battle*, pg. 93.
[86] 'De Gaulle Tells Ryan: I Like your book', *Sunday Independent*, 30th September 1962.
[87] 'My Longest Day', *Look* 10th June 1969.
[88] *The Kennedy Clan*, John H. Davis, pg. 250.
[89] *Making of the President 1960*, T. H. White.
[90] *Robert Kennedy and his Times*, Arthur Schlesinger, pg. 219.
[91] UPI press report dated 20th June 2004.
[92] *Don't Say Yes Until I Finish Talking*, Mel Gussow, pg. 218.
[93] David Ryan interview, 1st September 2004.
[94] 'Cornelius Ryan and the battle for the Kremlin Archives', Dominic Phelan, *History Ireland* May/June 2010.
[95] Ljubica Erickson interview, 31st August 2004.
[96] John Erickson obituary, *Daily Telegraph* 12th February 2002.
[97] *Captured by History*, John Toland, pg. 216.
[98] Gerard Ryan interview, 9th September 2004.
[99] 'JFK: TV's Defining Moment', *Irish Examiner*, 22nd November 2013.
[100] "The Last Battle' to be filmed', *Sunday Independent*, 2nd October 1966.
[101] *The Death of Adolf Hitler*, Lev Bezymenski, pg. 8.
[102] 'Apollo 11: How the world told the story', *Reader's Digest* October 1969.
[103] Contract held in Fulton Oursler Jr. archive, Georgetown University Library.
[104] Chicago radio interview with Bob Cromie, 1974.
[105] David Ryan interview, 1st September 2004.
[106] Walter Cronkite interview, 2nd December 2004.
[107] *A Private Battle*, pg. 38.
[108] David Ryan interview, 24th August 2004.
[109] Ryan script held at Dublin Writer's Museum.
[110] *A Private Battle,* pg. 285.
[111] *A Private Battle*, pg. 348.
[112] Walter Cronkite interview, 2nd December 2004.
[113] *A Private Battle*, pg. 362-370.
[114] 'I Got the Queen in the Morning and the Prince at Night', J. Anthony Lukas, *More*, November 1974, pg. 10.

[115] *Adventures in the Screen Trade*, William Goldman, pg. 278.
[116] 'After Cancer Claimed Cornelius Ryan, his Widow wrote of his Courage', *The New York Times* 29th June 1979.

Interviews:

I first became aware of Cornelius Ryan as an 'Irish writer' whilst working at the Dublin Writer's Museum in 1994 but what really surprised me was that an author who had sold millions of books was largely ignored by his home city.

Amazingly, I discovered that the writer's younger brother John lived only 15 minutes away from me and when we eventually met he turned out to be a real character – he even had a slight American accent as he had followed his famous brother to the United States in the 1950s. After that first interview he even apologised for not having any signed books for me to take away as he had lost them all playing poker!

Through John Ryan I was able to contact the other surviving brothers: David (in many ways the family's own unofficial historian); Gerard; a cousin also named John Ryan; and 90-year-old Elizabeth Ludlow – who, bizarrely, was not only the sister of Cornelius' best childhood friend but also lived in the Ryan's old house on Heytesbury Street. Sadly, all the Ryan brothers have since passed away (Gerard in 2006, John in 2013 and David in 2014) but their candid interviews form the backbone of this book.

During my research I was also lucky enough to get to talk to legendary American broadcaster Walter Cronkite about his wartime friend. My telephone interview with the then 88-year-old not only provided insights into their life as war reporters but was a real 'Did that really happen?' moment.

Doug McCabe, the archivist of the Cornelius Ryan Collection at the University of Ohio, was also a great source when it came to sorting fact from fiction in the Ryan story.

About the Author

Dominic Phelan was born in Dublin in 1972. He is the editor of the book *Cold War Space Sleuths* (Springer-Praxis 2013) and contributed a chapter to *Footprints in the Dust* (University of Nebraska Press, 2010).

Printed in Great Britain
by Amazon.co.uk, Ltd.,
Marston Gate.